Gnosis
Beyond the Veil of Illusion
Luiz Santos

Copyright © 2022 Luiz Santos
All rights reserved. No part of this book may be reproduced in any form or by any means without written permission from the copyright holder.
Cover image © Vellaz Studio
Review by Armando Vellaz
Graphic design by Amadeu Brumm
Layout by Matheus Costa
All rights reserved to:
Luiz A. Santos
Category: Gnosis

Summary

Prologue 4
Chapter 1 Gnostic Principles... 7
Chapter 2 Spiritual Preparation....................................... 15
Chapter 3 Gnostic Meditations 23
Chapter 4 Gnostic Self-Analysis...................................... 31
Chapter 5 Protection Rituals 39
Chapter 6 Chakra Alignment 47
Chapter 7 Initiation Rituals 55
Chapter 8 Creative Visualization 62
Chapter 9 Spiritual Healing... 71
Chapter 10 The Path of Wisdom..................................... 80
Chapter 11 Mysteries of the Demiurge 88
Chapter 12 Purification Rituals....................................... 96
Chapter 13 Inner Light Meditation 104
Chapter 14 Communication with the Higher Self.... 111
Chapter 15 Symbolism of the Arcanum...................... 119
Chapter 16 Inner Alchemy 127
Chapter 17 Dream Work 135
Chapter 18 Connection with Spiritual Entities 143
Chapter 19 Inner Silence Practices 152
Chapter 20 Liberation Ritual... 159
Chapter 21 Kundalini Energy 165
Chapter 22 The Art of Detachment.............................. 172
Chapter 23 Consciousness Expansion......................... 178
Chapter 24 The Path of the Heart................................ 184

Chapter 25 Gnostic Magic 190
Chapter 26 Integration of the Sacred 196
Chapter 27 Practice of Service 204
Chapter 28 Spiritual Ascension 211
Chapter 29 Journey Synthesis 218
Epilogue 224

Prologue

You, who now hold these pages, know that the moment you encountered this book was not a mere accident. There are encounters that transcend mere choice, that resonate in the deepest levels of the soul, carrying a kind of calling—a silent invitation to uncover something more. This is the invitation resting in your hands. You are about to enter a world where the invisible becomes tangible, where every symbol, every story, and every concept revealed pulses with a hidden truth, waiting for the right moment to surface.

The knowledge contained here, beyond words and paragraphs, harks back to the dawn of human spiritual seeking, an echo that resonates through creation myths and ancient legends. It is a call to awaken. Within these pages, you will not find doctrines, for the journey this work proposes requires much more: it requires your willingness to look inward, to explore the depths of your own beliefs and dreams.

Inside these pages, the material universe as you know it begins to reveal itself as a mask, a superficial layer that conceals the true brilliance behind it all. Gnosis, the term for this profound knowledge, is not merely knowing—it is feeling, perceiving what is eternal amid the ephemeral. Through concepts like the Demiurge, the imperfect creator shaping physical reality, and the Pleroma, the divine fullness from which all essence arises, you will come to see that the reality around you is, in its essence, not real. But what is this higher reality? And what does it mean to rediscover your own divinity, the spark that resides deep within you at this very moment?

You are about to embark on an experience of revelation. In Gnosticism, the concepts are not just distant ideas; they are gateways to the most authentic part of yourself. As you progress through each page, you will uncover the means to dissolve the illusions that keep you confined and explore the ancestral symbols that have inspired countless seekers before you. The figure of Sophia, embodiment of divine wisdom, will guide you on your journey. She, who descended into the material world to reunite with her origin in the Pleroma, also mirrors your spiritual path. Within you lies the same yearning, the same thirst for reunion with the divine. Each practice, each meditation, and each reflection are doorways that open up to this encounter.

Prepare yourself, for what you will find here is not a simple account of Gnosticism. It is a practical path, a route to transformation. The rituals of energetic purification, meditation techniques, and methods of self-inquiry described within these pages are tools for liberation and self-knowledge. As you advance, you will notice that the physical world as you perceive it becomes increasingly transparent, revealing the light that flows through it. This book was not written to explain; it was written to guide you, to lead you through the mysteries within your own soul.

As you delve into the depths of Gnostic teachings, you will hear the echo of something that has always been with you, an inner voice calling you home. This voice is Sophia's invitation, the promise that, by looking within, you will find the answer to every question and the meaning behind every symbol. On this path, you will discover that your own being is the gateway to understanding the universe.

Chapter 1
Gnostic Principles

Beneath the surface of ordinary perception lies a hidden world of symbols, secrets, and ineffable truths—an invitation to the seeker who dares to look beyond the ordinary. Gnosticism, at its core, isn't merely a philosophy; it's a journey into the deepest realms of self-knowledge, an unraveling of the veils that obscure the light of divinity within. The Gnostic tradition, centuries old yet timeless in essence, presents a map of spiritual liberation that promises to reveal the boundaries between illusion and truth, human and divine.

The journey into Gnostic understanding begins with fundamental concepts that orient the seeker: the Demiurge, the Pleroma, and the elusive notion of gnosis itself. These ideas speak of a cosmology that inverts common notions of creation and reality. Unlike many religious doctrines that celebrate the material world as divinely ordained, Gnosticism suggests that the visible world is a shadow—a construct shaped by the Demiurge, an imperfect creator whose limited nature has clouded the divine truth. In the Gnostic texts, the Demiurge, often depicted as a proud, ignorant being, oversees the material realm, exerting a kind of authority that binds humanity to illusions and separateness. This figure is both a creator and a deceiver, shaping reality but without true comprehension of the divine fullness, or Pleroma, that lies beyond.

The Pleroma, in contrast, is a realm of totality and unity, the very essence of divine completeness. It exists beyond the limitations of form, a pure and radiant state from which all beings arise but few can remember. The journey of Gnosticism is one of rediscovery, of awakening to the knowledge that our true nature lies not within the material, but within this boundless spiritual fullness. To know the Pleroma is to know oneself at the deepest level, to perceive life as an unfolding of divine potential rather than a series of finite, disconnected experiences.

Central to this tradition is the figure of Sophia, a divine emanation who embodies the archetype of wisdom and the soul's profound longing for reunion with the divine. In myth, Sophia descends from the Pleroma, embodying both the spark of divine truth and the capacity for suffering. Her story reflects the journey of every seeker, a tale of loss, separation, and the eventual aspiration toward reunion with the divine. Sophia's fall into the material world mirrors the condition of humanity, yet her longing to return to the Source becomes an inspiration for those on the Gnostic path. She is the reminder that, despite the layers of illusion, the divine essence remains within, patiently awaiting our awakening.

Gnosticism offers a lens through which to see the world as a duality—the material realm with its fleeting forms, and the spiritual essence that stands immutable beyond it. In Gnostic thought, to live solely for the material is to be caught in the Demiurge's web, bound by illusions and limitations that obstruct the perception of the higher reality. Yet, through gnosis, an experiential knowledge that transcends ordinary understanding, the seeker can begin to see through these illusions. Gnosis is not a mere accumulation of facts or doctrines; it is a deep, inner knowing that comes from direct communion with the divine essence within oneself. This kind of knowledge is profoundly transformative, offering freedom from the limitations of the material realm and leading the seeker into an expanded consciousness.

Historical texts form the foundation of this mystical path, documents like the Gospel of Thomas, The Pistis Sophia, and The Apocryphon of John, which emerged in the early centuries of Christianity. These writings do not prescribe rigid doctrines;

rather, they serve as signposts pointing the way toward an individual journey of enlightenment. Each text holds the echoes of ancient voices that urge the reader to look within, to find the divine spark hidden beneath layers of conditioning and illusion. The teachings found within these texts are subversive, questioning established religious structures and challenging the notion of a purely benevolent creator who commands absolute authority over reality.

At its heart, Gnosticism is deeply experiential. The teachings emphasize personal insight and inner discovery rather than blind adherence to external authorities. This tradition encourages each seeker to embark on an individual quest, to encounter the divine directly rather than relying on intermediaries. In this, Gnosticism stands as a path of spiritual autonomy, where each step is a revelation, each practice a shedding of the unnecessary layers that obscure the divine essence within. It is a call to seek truth in its purest form, to transcend the limitations imposed by the physical senses and the conditioned mind.

The figure of the Demiurge, often misunderstood as purely malevolent, represents the imperfect nature of the material realm—a world that is real enough to be experienced but not truly "real" in the ultimate sense. It is a creation born of limitation, and thus it cannot fully capture the boundlessness of the divine. In Gnostic terms, the material realm is a kind of prison, a construct that separates humanity from its true nature. Yet, this prison is not unbreakable; through practices of meditation, self-inquiry, and spiritual exercises, the seeker can begin to unravel the illusion, to pierce through the shadows and glimpse the Pleroma beyond.

The Gnostic journey begins in earnest with the realization that the material world, as alluring as it may be, is transient and filled with illusions. It is a place of learning, where the soul undergoes a process of refinement and awakening. The sufferings and challenges of earthly life are not mere accidents but reflections of the soul's journey to remember its true nature. Through gnosis, the seeker starts to see beyond the surface, recognizing the divine spark within and the interconnectedness of all beings. The material realm, with all its imperfections, becomes a mirror through which the soul glimpses its own potential, learning to transcend and ultimately to integrate the experience.

As the reader embarks on this exploration of Gnostic principles, they are invited to step into a deeper awareness, to contemplate the nature of reality beyond appearances. This first chapter is only an entry point, an initiation into a world where knowledge is sacred and each insight is a step closer to the divine. Through Gnostic practices, the seeker learns to cultivate an inner silence, a receptivity to wisdom that lies beyond thought. In the stillness, Sophia's voice whispers, a reminder of the divine wisdom that each soul carries within, awaiting rediscovery.

This journey is one of liberation—not from life, but from the constraints of an illusory existence. Gnosticism invites the seeker to awaken from the dream of separateness, to recognize the oneness that underlies all things. Each practice, each meditation, and each reflection deepens the seeker's connection with the divine within, transforming the world from a place of entrapment into a sacred space of awakening. Here, at the threshold of gnosis, the journey begins, promising revelations that are both profound and profoundly transformative.

The path of the Gnostic is one of depths upon depths, an endless peeling away of illusions to reveal truths that, while challenging, promise a liberation that few other paths offer. As the seeker delves further into the principles of Gnosticism, a world unfolds that is both strange and compelling, filled with symbols, myths, and archetypes that speak not just to the intellect, but to the very soul. The journey becomes one of feeling and understanding, a dance with the numinous, where each story and figure becomes a mirror reflecting hidden facets of the self.

Among these mysterious figures stands Sophia, the embodiment of divine wisdom, her presence a guide through the labyrinth of spirit. Her tale, layered with meaning and complexity, speaks to the Gnostic journey's inherent longing and suffering, where wisdom must be wrested from the jaws of confusion.

Sophia's fall from the Pleroma—a descent from purity to the imperfect material world—resonates deeply, for her story echoes the journey of the human soul. Separated from the Source, she falls into a realm of limitations and illusions, where she becomes both guide and reminder of the wisdom that lies dormant within each seeker.

Sophia's yearning for reunion with the divine ignites a similar yearning within those who follow the Gnostic path, where inner knowledge, or gnosis, becomes a way to reconnect with the forgotten, radiant essence. This wisdom doesn't come easily; it must be uncovered in the midst of life's trials and obscurities, requiring a willingness to look beyond appearances. For the Gnostic, Sophia is not simply a myth but a living archetype of inner wisdom, a guide through darkness who knows both the taste of despair and the light of redemption.

As Gnosticism took root in different lands and epochs, it branched into various schools of thought, each adding layers of interpretation and practice. The Sethian school, for instance, focuses on the figure of Seth, a being who represents the line of humanity's divine inheritance, a lineage tracing back to Adam but set apart from the masses. Sethians see the material world as a construct designed to obscure the truth of the Pleroma, with the Demiurge casting veils of illusion to trap the soul. Their practices are often contemplative, seeking knowledge of higher realms through ritual, meditation, and symbolic stories. The Valentinians, on the other hand, bring a nuanced interpretation of Gnostic myths, often merging Christian elements with Gnostic thought, portraying the Demiurge as less a tyrant and more a misguided creator. Their rituals emphasize divine love and the redemption of both spirit and matter, aiming to transform the material world through the power of gnosis.

Each school holds a unique vision, yet all point to a reality beyond the senses, a place where the soul sheds its bindings and reclaims its divine heritage. These variations remind the seeker that Gnosticism is not a static doctrine, but a living tradition—adaptable, questioning, and deeply individual. Every symbol, every myth, serves as a doorway into the vast inner landscape of the soul, urging the seeker to find truth within rather than in external authorities.

Symbolism holds a place of great importance in the Gnostic journey, functioning as both a key and a veil. Symbols within Gnosticism—such as the serpent, the lion-faced Demiurge, and the divine light—carry layers of meaning, each interpretation pointing to another level of understanding. The serpent, reviled in orthodox interpretations of the Eden myth, becomes in some Gnostic texts a bearer of knowledge, a figure who offers humanity the fruit of awareness. The serpent's wisdom is both liberating and dangerous, as it invites the soul to question, to see beyond the confines of imposed beliefs. In this way, Gnosticism often turns traditional symbols on their head, offering an alternative view that invites the seeker to reexamine inherited assumptions and find their own truth.

The concept of gnosis itself becomes more nuanced as the seeker advances. Gnosis is not intellectual knowledge but a direct, often ineffable awareness of one's divine origin, a knowing that transforms rather than informs. This experiential knowledge may arise in moments of meditation, through encounters with beauty, or in deep, introspective silence. It is both a remembering and an awakening, a stirring of the soul that recalls its origins in the Pleroma, beyond the limitations of time and form. Such gnosis is elusive, for it cannot be taught in words or captured in doctrines; it must be experienced, felt, and integrated, becoming part of one's very being.

The journey of gnosis challenges the seeker to reconcile the dualities within: the material and the spiritual, the human and the divine, the self and the cosmos. This process often requires a confrontation with the self, a rigorous self-examination that lays bare the illusions, desires, and fears that cloud the soul's vision. The seeker becomes both alchemist and alchemical matter, transforming themselves through practices of meditation, inner silence, and sacred ritual. Each of these practices is a way of peeling away the layers of conditioning and illusion, gradually revealing the clear light of the divine spark within.

As the reader engages with these deepening principles, they are called to cultivate a reverence for mystery, to hold the paradoxes of existence without seeking to resolve them. Gnosticism doesn't offer easy answers; instead, it provides a framework within which each individual can explore their own questions, guided by the symbols and stories that resonate with their unique journey. In this way, Gnosticism remains profoundly relevant, speaking to those who feel that there is more to reality than what meets the eye, to those who yearn for a truth that transcends doctrine and dogma.

The seeker of gnosis is often likened to a wanderer, one who must learn to navigate the realms of both light and shadow, to discern the true from the false within themselves and the world. This journey requires courage, for it involves facing the illusions that the Demiurge has woven, recognizing the ways in which they have internalized these limitations and mistaken them for reality. The figure of Sophia serves as both an ally and a reminder that wisdom is not found in escape but in integration, in the ability to hold the light of the Pleroma within the constraints of the material form.

In the depths of this exploration, the seeker may come to understand that the Demiurge itself is a mirror, a reflection of their own limited perceptions. By confronting this figure within, by questioning and dissolving the boundaries it represents, the seeker draws closer to the experience of gnosis, an opening into the infinite. This realization is not the end of the journey but a new beginning, a threshold into even greater mysteries.

Through these principles, the Gnostic path becomes a way of awakening to the sacred within the self, a path that honors the individual's right to find their own truth. It is a journey of courage and insight, where each discovery brings the seeker closer to the luminous truth of their own divine essence. To walk this path is to become a student of mystery, a friend of Sophia, and a seeker of gnosis—a timeless journey that forever invites the soul into a deeper, more profound understanding of itself and the universe it inhabits.

Chapter 2
Spiritual Preparation

The journey into Gnostic practice calls for an inner stillness, a quiet foundation upon which the soul may stand as it embarks on its ascent through hidden realms and ancient mysteries. In this phase, the seeker must attend to the clearing of mind and spirit, crafting an environment that nourishes receptivity to gnosis and prepares the ground for a sacred life. Spiritual preparation is essential, for without it, the practices to come may become obscured, entangled in the distractions of the untrained mind and the cluttered energies that naturally surround human life.

Breathing becomes the first step—a simple yet transformative act that shifts awareness from the ordinary to the sacred. Gnostic breathing techniques emphasize intentional inhalations and exhalations, directing attention inward and helping the practitioner cultivate presence. By focusing on the breath, the mind begins to calm, like the surface of a lake settling after a storm. These breaths are slow, deep, and mindful, each one drawing the seeker closer to an inner silence. This silence is not emptiness; rather, it is a receptive state, one that invites the wisdom of the soul to rise from its depths, unclouded by surface thoughts.

Alongside breathwork, the practitioner is guided in the art of energy purification, an approach that clears the residual energies of the external world. Living in the material realm exposes the individual to various influences, some positive, others draining. This energy, like dust settling on the body, accumulates over time and can create disturbances in the psyche, disrupting focus and intuition. Techniques of energy purification begin with simple visualizations—imagining light coursing through the body, washing away heaviness and tension. As the light flows, it brings clarity and renewal, reawakening the body's natural harmony and balance.

But more than the inner landscape must be attended to; the physical space around the seeker must also be consecrated, transformed into a sanctuary for self-exploration. The Gnostic tradition values the creation of sacred space, understanding it as both a physical and spiritual undertaking. The seeker might choose a dedicated corner in their home, a space that is free from distractions, clean, and decorated with symbols that inspire introspection. Objects like candles, crystals, or symbolic icons become anchors, reminders of the intentions set forth in this sacred work.

Cleansing rituals can be performed to sanctify the chosen space. A simple method involves lighting a candle or burning sage, using the smoke to purify the room and create an atmosphere conducive to meditation and reflection. These actions, while external, echo deeply within, resonating with the soul's need for a quiet, untouched space. Each aspect of the ritual reinforces the boundary between the sacred and the mundane, allowing the practitioner to fully immerse themselves in the work of gnosis. As the air fills with the scent of sage or incense, the mind becomes primed for deeper connection, its defenses lowered, its attention sharpened.

Once the environment is purified, the practitioner moves to the practice of visualization, an exercise that blends focus with creative imagination. Visualization serves as a bridge between the conscious and subconscious, a method that connects the seeker with symbols and archetypes that will play a central role in the Gnostic journey. One might imagine themselves standing in a circle of light, surrounded by protective energy that guards them against disturbances from the external world. This circle is a place of refuge, a space where the divine spark within can be nurtured and brought to the forefront of consciousness.

With these practices, the reader begins to notice a shift, a subtle movement from distraction toward presence. The mind, which often flits from thought to thought, starts to settle, creating space for clarity and insight. A calm mind is essential for the path ahead, for the Gnostic journey requires sustained attention and openness. Just as an artist needs a clear canvas, so too does the seeker need an uncluttered mind, free from the noise of daily life, to receive the inner whispers of Sophia, the divine wisdom within.

The preparation phase is not merely a preliminary step but a practice in itself, one that the seeker returns to again and again. As they breathe, visualize, and cleanse their space, they are reminded of their intentions, reconnected with the purpose of their journey. Each breath becomes an affirmation of commitment, each gesture a symbol of dedication to the path of self-knowledge and spiritual liberation. The seeker becomes accustomed to this ritual of preparation, learning to find stillness in the most basic acts, such as sitting in silence, breathing with awareness, or lighting a candle with intention.

Gradually, these simple acts of preparation become a doorway into deeper states of awareness. Through them, the practitioner gains control over their inner environment, learning to hold their focus despite external chaos or distraction. This is essential in the Gnostic path, where encounters with the divine are often subtle, requiring a level of sensitivity that can only emerge from a practiced and disciplined mind. In learning to quiet the surface mind, the practitioner opens channels to deeper insights, creating space for the divine to speak.

The benefits of this preparation extend beyond ritual and meditation; they flow into daily life, affecting interactions, perceptions, and responses. The purified mind becomes less reactive, more discerning. Patterns of thought that once distracted the seeker gradually fade, replaced by a grounded sense of purpose and clarity. This mental clarity is not an end in itself, but a tool that allows the seeker to engage more deeply with the teachings and practices to come.

As the seeker deepens in these preliminary practices, they may notice an increased sensitivity to energy, an awareness that goes beyond physical sensation. This sensitivity is a gift, a subtle shift in consciousness that allows for a fuller experience of the practices that will follow. The seeker begins to sense energy flows within the body and the surrounding environment, learning to recognize the natural rhythms that influence thoughts, emotions, and spiritual awareness. These perceptions become a guide, showing the practitioner how to tune into the ebb and flow of life itself, aligning with the divine rhythm that underlies all things.

Preparation, then, is not a mere prologue to the spiritual work of Gnosticism; it is the foundation upon which all future practices rest. Each breath, each cleansing ritual, each act of visualization builds the inner sanctuary where gnosis can take root and flourish. The seeker learns to trust in this process, finding comfort in the routine and rhythm of preparation, which brings them closer to their divine essence.

In time, these practices will become second nature, woven into the fabric of daily life, creating a seamless connection between the sacred and the mundane. The reader, now a practitioner, finds that the physical space they once consecrated is only a reflection of an inner sanctuary that can be accessed anywhere, at any moment. This inner sanctuary becomes a place of solace, a wellspring of strength and insight, a testament to the power of preparation in the journey toward self-knowledge and spiritual liberation.

With the foundation of spiritual preparation set, the Gnostic practitioner is called to deepen these practices, engaging in the art of purifying both the seen and unseen realms of their life. This stage goes beyond the initial steps of breathing, cleansing, and focusing. It moves toward creating a refined energetic environment where the spirit can rest and awaken, and where the voice of inner wisdom might rise more clearly. Every action now becomes an act of devotion, a bridge connecting the mundane with the sacred.

The purification ritual becomes more intricate, now incorporating sacred elements from the natural world, such as herbs known for their cleansing qualities. Ancient Gnostic practitioners, like many spiritual seekers, turned to the earth's gifts for purifying the energy field. Herbs like sage, rosemary, and lavender are burned, filling the air with fragrant smoke that seems to dissolve lingering energies. This ritual, known as "smudging," is done slowly, with intent, as the practitioner moves through their sacred space. The smoke purifies, lifting away the remnants of thoughts, emotions, and energies that may have gathered in the environment.

Each herb carries its own unique vibration, and learning to work with these energies becomes a form of communion with nature itself. For example, sage is seen as a purifier of heavy energies, suitable for spaces that feel dense or disturbed. Rosemary, associated with clarity and protection, is burned to shield the practitioner from outside interference. Lavender, with its calming qualities, is chosen for practices of inner peace and relaxation. Through such herbs, the practitioner invites the essence of the natural world into their sacred space, aligning with the rhythms of the earth as a means of attuning to the higher realms.

Beyond herbs, cleansing baths also become a significant ritual in this deeper preparation. These baths, often infused with salts, herbs, or essential oils, act as a full-body purification, soothing both body and spirit. The salt in the water works as a grounding agent, drawing out heavy energies and leaving the practitioner feeling lighter, more connected to their core essence. With the herbs floating in the water or the aroma of essential oils rising, the bath becomes an immersion into a tranquil, meditative state. It is a return to the simplicity of water, an element revered in countless spiritual traditions for its power to cleanse, renew, and transform.

As the practitioner learns to purify their personal space and body, the concept of the altar arises—a personal center of focus, a grounding place where rituals, reflections, and meditations take place. Creating an altar is not a matter of decoration but an invitation to align with the divine. This space may hold sacred objects such as candles, crystals, symbols, or a personal item with deep meaning, each chosen with intention. A candle, for instance, represents the eternal flame of gnosis, while crystals like clear quartz amplify energy, creating a clearer channel for insights. The practitioner arranges these objects thoughtfully, intuitively, honoring them as both symbols and energetic tools.

Once the altar is arranged, the act of consecration follows—a ritual dedicated to imbuing these objects with sacred intent. Consecration is performed through focused intention, a quiet prayer, or a mantra that speaks to the purpose of the space. In the Gnostic tradition, mantras carry a powerful resonance, serving to invoke protection, clarity, and connection. As the practitioner recites their chosen words, they visualize a gentle light enveloping each item, blessing it and charging it with the energy necessary for spiritual work. These items become more than physical objects; they transform into conduits of the sacred, companions on the journey.

Protection mantras are then introduced as an essential practice to maintain a high vibrational state and shield the practitioner from interference. Gnosticism teaches that the unseen world is populated by various forces, some beneficial and others disruptive. Through the use of protective mantras, the practitioner fortifies their aura, establishing a boundary between themselves and any energies that do not align with their purpose. These mantras, often simple yet profound, are repeated with devotion, each word resonating through the practitioner's being, creating an armor of light around them.

The concept of a personal sanctuary expands, no longer limited to a particular space or time. The sanctuary now becomes portable, a sacred atmosphere that the practitioner can carry with them wherever they go. This state of inner sanctuary is nurtured through consistent practice, where the rituals of purification, consecration, and protection reinforce the boundary between the self and the external world. The practitioner learns to invoke this sanctuary even in the busiest of spaces, holding a piece of the sacred within them, regardless of external circumstances.

These practices, while powerful on their own, deepen when they are repeated regularly, becoming a part of the practitioner's daily rhythm. Morning or evening rituals might involve lighting a candle, reciting a mantra, or spending a few moments in stillness before the altar. The consistency of these practices weaves an unseen layer of stability around the practitioner's life, grounding them and keeping them attuned to the divine within. With each repetition, the body, mind, and spirit come to recognize these rituals as a signal for inner quiet, a space where they can release the burdens of daily life.

As the practitioner strengthens their preparation, they may begin to feel a shift in their perception. Ordinary events may take on a new significance, as if imbued with hidden layers of meaning. The quieting of external distractions brings an awareness of the interconnectedness of all things, a subtle perception of the divine presence in everyday life. In this purified state, insights begin to arise unbidden—a deeper awareness of the self, a sense of unity with the world, and moments of profound clarity that hint at the path ahead.

By creating a sacred space both within and without, the seeker opens themselves to the mysteries of gnosis. The spirit, now unburdened, can access the quiet wisdom that resides beneath the surface mind, a wisdom that grows with each ritual, each prayer, and each breath. This spiritual preparation transforms the seeker, aligning their entire being with the divine, setting the stage for the deeper practices that lie ahead on the Gnostic path.

Through these acts of devotion, the practitioner is no longer merely preparing—they are already within the journey, attuning to the rhythm of the sacred. In each mantra, each consecrated object, and each breath of purified air, they touch a timeless reality, experiencing an echo of the divine fullness that Gnosticism calls the Pleroma. With this foundation, the soul is ready to explore the further reaches of inner light, where mysteries await and gnosis unfolds.

Chapter 3
Gnostic Meditations

To step into Gnostic meditation is to enter a realm where the silence of the mind becomes a doorway to deeper truths. These meditations are not mere exercises in relaxation; they are deliberate practices of self-knowledge, paths that reveal hidden layers of consciousness and clear the way for gnosis. In these moments, the seeker quiets the outer world, turning inward to connect with the essence that lies beyond the mundane, reaching for the spark of the divine within.

The foundation of Gnostic meditation begins with concentration, an art of focusing the mind on a single point, refining attention until it becomes steady as a flame undisturbed by the wind. For many, this journey begins with something as simple as focusing on the breath. Each inhale draws the practitioner inward, each exhale grounds them deeper into the present. This rhythmic pattern gradually silences the endless cascade of thoughts that usually occupy the mind, creating a tranquil space within. Concentration on the breath is a gateway, an initiation into self-awareness where the seeker learns to observe rather than be swept away by the mind's habitual wanderings.

As the breath becomes an anchor, the practitioner next engages in a practice of inner listening, where the senses, usually directed outward, are turned within. In this quiet, they encounter the subtle stirrings of their inner self—a soft, elusive presence that often goes unnoticed amid the noise of daily life. This inner self, or divine spark, is the very essence that Gnostic teachings seek to awaken. In listening without expectation, the practitioner finds that silence itself has a language, one that reveals truths beyond words, bringing flashes of insight, hints of the vast spiritual depth within.

To deepen concentration, the seeker is encouraged to use a simple yet powerful tool: a mantra. A Gnostic mantra is a word or phrase imbued with spiritual resonance, often derived from ancient texts or languages, designed to evoke a specific frequency within the soul. Mantras like "Sophia" or "Pleroma" are chosen for their connection to divine wisdom and fullness, essential concepts in Gnosticism. The mantra is repeated softly, either aloud or in silence, synchronizing with the breath. With each repetition, the mantra takes on a life of its own, becoming a bridge that draws the practitioner closer to their true self, calming the restless mind and opening the heart to the mysteries of existence.

Beyond concentration, the practice of contemplation brings the seeker into a direct engagement with profound Gnostic concepts. Contemplation differs from concentration in that it invites the practitioner to hold a theme or image in mind, allowing it to unfold within the psyche. Here, the seeker may contemplate the concept of the Demiurge, the imperfect creator of the material world, or the Pleroma, the realm of divine fullness. Such contemplation is not an intellectual exercise; it is an open, receptive stance, one that allows these symbols to reveal their meaning intuitively, reaching the depths of the soul rather than remaining in the mind.

The practitioner might choose to contemplate an image—a candle flame symbolizing inner light, or a reflective surface that represents the truth behind illusions. By focusing on such symbols, they begin to perceive the layers of meaning embedded within each one. The candle, for instance, becomes more than a source of light; it becomes a reminder of the inner divine spark, a flame that burns within, illuminating even the darkest corners of the psyche. This imagery, like a key, unlocks a door within the subconscious, leading the seeker into an understanding that words alone could never convey.

As the practice of Gnostic meditation unfolds, the seeker learns to embrace the art of self-observation. In this state, they are both participant and observer, experiencing thoughts and emotions without identifying with them. This detachment does not mean indifference; rather, it allows the practitioner to see their patterns of thought and behavior from a place of clarity, unclouded by judgment. The mind is like a still pond, and in this stillness, they can observe their reflections—fears, desires, and the attachments that bind them to the material world. Each observation, each insight, becomes a step toward inner freedom, a dismantling of the false identities constructed by the ego.

Self-observation reveals the transient nature of thoughts and emotions, the realization that what often feels like a fixed "self" is in fact a constantly shifting collection of experiences. With this insight, the seeker begins to loosen their identification with these shifting aspects, recognizing that beneath it all lies a steady, unchanging presence—a quiet witness, an aspect of the self that is intimately connected with the divine. This witness is not swayed by the dramas of life; it remains a calm, silent observer, present in each moment, guiding the seeker closer to gnosis.

In moments of stillness, when the mind has quieted and the self-observation becomes seamless, a new layer of awareness emerges. Here, the practitioner may experience the first glimpses of a deeper reality, a fleeting but profound sense of interconnectedness with all things. The boundaries that once seemed solid—between self and other, inner and outer—begin to blur. This is the beginning of gnosis, a direct knowing that transcends intellectual understanding and enters the realm of spiritual perception. It is an awakening to the realization that the self, in its essence, is not separate from the divine; it is a part of the sacred unity that underlies all of existence.

The fruits of these meditation practices are subtle, often unfolding gradually, like petals of a hidden flower opening to the light. Patience is essential, for these glimpses of gnosis cannot be forced. The seeker learns to trust in the process, allowing each meditation to work its subtle transformations. With each session, the mind becomes more accustomed to stillness, the inner self more receptive to insight. Gradually, the noise of ordinary consciousness fades, replaced by a quiet, spacious awareness where the deeper truths of Gnosticism can reveal themselves.

These meditation practices are not an end in themselves; they are doorways, tools that prepare the mind and spirit for the profound work of the Gnostic path. The seeker comes to realize that each practice, each moment of silence, each breath, is part of a sacred rhythm, a timeless dance that leads them closer to their divine origin. In this space of meditation, they encounter the mysteries of the self, the veiled wisdom of Sophia, and the light of the Pleroma shining through the layers of the material world.

As these practices take root, the practitioner begins to embody the qualities of inner peace, clarity, and a quiet strength that serves them in all aspects of life. The awareness cultivated in meditation extends beyond the practice itself, influencing thoughts, actions, and relationships, aligning the seeker's outer life with their inner journey. The path of Gnostic meditation becomes a lifelong journey, a continual unfolding of layers, drawing the soul ever closer to its divine essence, to the unity that is both the source and the goal of all spiritual seeking.

The second part of Gnostic meditation unfolds into deeper, more intricate practices, inviting the seeker to journey beyond self-awareness into realms of expanded consciousness. Here, meditation becomes not only a discipline but a mystical process, a means of directly encountering the subtle, sacred forces that lie within and around us. These advanced techniques reach beyond calming the mind; they invite the practitioner to pierce the veil of the material world and step into direct communion with the divine.

Visualization emerges as a powerful tool in this expanded phase. Unlike earlier practices that focused on centering awareness and observing the mind, visualization invites the practitioner to actively shape their inner reality. This practice begins with creating mental images that resonate deeply with Gnostic symbols and teachings. The seeker might visualize a brilliant inner light at the heart center, a sacred flame that represents the divine spark, eternally burning within. As they deepen their focus, this flame begins to grow, illuminating the mind and body with warmth and clarity. Through such imagery, the practitioner connects to an essential truth—that the divine light is not distant or external, but part of their innermost being.

This light then becomes the focal point of a practice that calls on each energy center, or chakra, to awaken to higher states of consciousness. Beginning at the base of the spine, the seeker directs their awareness upwards, visualizing the light rising slowly through each energy center: from the roots of their being, through the heart, and finally to the crown of the head, where it radiates outward. As each center opens to the light, it brings clarity, healing, and an expanded sense of awareness. This method serves not only to balance the energies within the body but also to awaken a perception that transcends the ordinary senses, a Gnostic insight into the unity between the physical self and the divine essence.

As visualization practices become more refined, the seeker learns to integrate the use of mantras specific to the Gnostic tradition. These mantras, sacred syllables or phrases often taken from ancient texts, create vibrational frequencies that resonate with higher states of awareness. Mantras such as "Ain Soph" or "Sophia" are spoken softly or internally, synchronizing with the breath and the rhythm of the meditation. The vibrations of these sounds become carriers of intention, each word a call to the divine. Spoken with reverence, the mantra gradually shifts the state of consciousness, dissolving boundaries and attuning the practitioner to the universal resonance of the Pleroma, the divine fullness.

Alongside visualization and mantras, guided meditations enter the practice, allowing the seeker to explore symbolic realms and spiritual archetypes. A guided journey might begin with the image of a staircase, each step leading downward into a quiet, hidden sanctuary within the soul. This sanctuary is a sacred space—a reflection of the divine realms, rich with symbols and mythic imagery that echo Gnostic teachings. Here, the seeker might encounter Sophia, the divine wisdom, not merely as an idea but as a living presence. This inner journey, aided by visualization, connects the seeker with the archetypes of Gnosticism, imbuing them with a profound sense of presence, connection, and purpose.

Each guided meditation is carefully structured to engage not only the mind but the heart, inviting the practitioner to feel the resonance of these symbols deeply. Encountering Sophia, for example, is not a mere mental exercise but an opportunity to experience divine wisdom as a presence within. The figure of Sophia becomes a mirror, a reminder of the inner wisdom that lies waiting to be awakened. Through these symbolic encounters, the seeker gains insights that transcend rational thought, entering into the realm of spiritual intuition, where knowledge is felt rather than comprehended.

In addition to these symbolic encounters, advanced Gnostic meditations introduce the practice of ascension meditation, a technique that involves directing awareness beyond the material plane into realms of pure consciousness. Ascension meditation begins with grounding the body, bringing attention to the breath, and focusing the mind. From this stable foundation, the seeker imagines lifting their awareness upward, visualizing a journey through layers of light. They rise through realms of increasing purity, each one bringing them closer to the divine Source. At the peak of this meditation, they may experience a fleeting but profound connection with the Pleroma, a moment of pure being where the soul feels both separate from and unified with all things.

This elevated state, often accompanied by a sense of boundless love and peace, marks an encounter with gnosis itself—a direct, experiential knowing that cannot be fully described but only felt. In these moments, the seeker grasps intuitively that the material world, with all its limitations, is but a fragment of a much greater whole. The soul feels an unmistakable pull toward this higher reality, an invitation to remember its true origin and purpose. This experience of ascension shifts the practitioner's understanding of their own existence, revealing the divine nature that lies beneath the surface of everyday awareness.

In the silence that follows, the seeker is encouraged to meditate on their experience, to let the insight settle into the depths of their being. These moments of connection, though fleeting, leave a lasting imprint, subtly transforming the practitioner's perception of themselves and the world around them. Each encounter with this higher state serves as a reminder of the divine essence within, a source of strength and clarity that can be drawn upon in daily life.

Another advanced practice is the recapitulation meditation, a form of reflection that allows the seeker to review their day or recent experiences with a Gnostic perspective. In this meditation, they recall events, emotions, and interactions, observing them from a detached and reflective state. This practice reveals patterns, emotional responses, and hidden motivations, all of which serve as obstacles or aids on the path to gnosis. Recapitulation helps the practitioner to purify the psyche, shedding attachments and aligning more closely with their true self. By examining life with a clear and compassionate gaze, they begin to see each moment as part of a divine tapestry, an opportunity for growth and understanding.

Through these meditative practices, the practitioner begins to glimpse the potential of the Gnostic path—not merely as a series of techniques but as a transformative way of being. The quiet realizations that arise in meditation, the resonance of a mantra, the vivid imagery of a guided journey, and the detachment fostered by self-reflection all serve to reveal layers of self that were previously hidden. Gnostic meditation, then, becomes a means of liberation, a way to transcend the illusions of separateness and touch the heart of unity.

With each session, the inner world becomes more familiar, a landscape where sacred encounters and profound insights reside. The seeker begins to trust in the process, learning to navigate the realms of light and shadow within, holding both in balance. The practice of Gnostic meditation grows into a lifelong journey, one that continues to reveal new layers, new mysteries, and deeper truths as the soul draws closer to the light of the Pleroma.

In time, the experiences of meditation flow naturally into the rest of life. The quiet gained in meditation extends into daily interactions, bringing a calmness that reflects a deeper awareness. Challenges are faced with clarity, and moments of beauty or connection become gateways to the divine. The seeker walks through life with a new sense of purpose, each step taken with the knowledge that they are not merely traversing the material world but engaging in a sacred dance with the divine within and beyond.

This is the gift of Gnostic meditation—a practice that offers not only peace but profound transformation, an awakening to the boundless light that lies at the core of all existence.

Chapter 4
Gnostic Self-Analysis

The path of Gnostic self-analysis begins with an invitation: to step into the shadowed halls of the inner world, to confront and comprehend the self's depths. This practice isn't merely one of introspection; it is an act of unveiling, a search for clarity amidst the layers of habit, fear, and inherited beliefs. Gnostic self-analysis calls the practitioner to study their own mind, emotions, and patterns, casting light on those forces that govern action yet remain unseen.

In this first approach to self-analysis, the seeker learns the foundational tools of self-observation and self-questioning, establishing a discipline of reflective awareness. This process begins with setting aside time each day to simply observe one's own thoughts and emotional responses, without judgment or interference. During these moments, the seeker becomes a witness, cultivating an internal gaze that separates their true essence from the constant stream of thoughts and reactions. Observing the mind in this way, the practitioner soon sees that what they might usually call "self" is a mix of thoughts, emotions, memories, and attachments. To reach gnosis, one must learn to look beyond these shifting aspects and find the steady awareness that observes them.

The practice of self-questioning follows, a technique designed to penetrate deeper into the layers of the psyche, unraveling the roots of patterns that shape one's experience. In Gnostic tradition, self-questioning is not about self-criticism but about asking sincere questions that lead to clarity. The seeker might ask, "What is the origin of this desire?" or "Why do I react with fear or anger in certain situations?" These questions are like keys that unlock doors within, revealing long-hidden motivations, beliefs, and emotional responses that shape daily behavior and even spiritual perception.

In this process, the practitioner is likely to encounter recurring patterns—ways of thinking and behaving that appear repeatedly in life. These patterns, which often operate unconsciously, are barriers on the Gnostic path, veiling the truth of one's divine nature. For instance, the seeker may discover a habitual tendency to seek approval, driven by a deeply rooted fear of rejection. Or they may notice a pattern of anger that emerges in response to perceived injustices, pointing to a need to control or change others. Recognizing these patterns is a first step; it brings them into awareness, where they can be observed without judgment, allowing the seeker to move beyond automatic reactions and toward conscious choice.

This practice of self-analysis reveals that much of what the individual believes to be "self" is, in fact, a construction shaped by societal influences, past experiences, and inherited beliefs. Gnosticism encourages the seeker to see beyond this constructed self, to identify the soul beneath these layers of conditioning. This deeper self is often silent, an observing presence that holds neither judgment nor attachment. Through regular self-observation, the practitioner begins to glimpse this pure awareness, discovering a space within where clarity and peace reside undisturbed.

To aid in this work, the Gnostic practitioner may keep a daily record, a journal where thoughts, emotions, and reflections are documented. This written record becomes a mirror, a way of seeing oneself from the outside, revealing insights that might otherwise be overlooked. For instance, patterns begin to emerge in writing that were invisible in the moment. What seemed like isolated events or emotions reveal themselves as interconnected expressions of deeper beliefs. Each entry, however brief, builds a bridge between the conscious and subconscious, allowing the seeker to bring hidden aspects of self into awareness.

Self-analysis, however, is not an easy or comfortable process. The deeper one goes, the more they encounter those parts of themselves that are often resisted or denied. This confrontation with the shadow—the repressed fears, desires, and unresolved emotions—is both challenging and liberating. For the Gnostic, these shadows are not enemies to be defeated; they are aspects of self that have simply not yet been brought into harmony. By facing them with courage, the practitioner begins the work of integration, acknowledging these parts without judgment or fear, seeing them as essential pieces of the larger self.

A further technique in this process is the practice of detachment, learning to observe the emotions and thoughts that arise without identifying with them. Detachment, however, is not a form of suppression; rather, it is a way of creating space between awareness and experience, allowing the practitioner to see emotions as transient phenomena rather than fixed aspects of the self. This perspective frees the seeker from the grip of emotional responses, enabling them to act from a place of calm, rather than from reaction.

This first stage of self-analysis also introduces the role of memory as a tool for self-discovery. By examining key memories, the practitioner can uncover formative experiences that have shaped their perceptions and behaviors. This is not a quest to relive the past but to understand its influence. Certain memories, when observed with detachment, reveal the origins of current patterns, providing insight into how past experiences shape present reactions. The Gnostic practitioner reflects on these memories with an open heart, seeking understanding rather than dwelling on pain or regret.

As the practitioner continues, they may experience moments of clarity, insights that arise spontaneously during self-reflection or meditation. These insights come unbidden, yet they feel like pieces of a puzzle falling into place, revealing an expanded understanding of self. Such insights are gifts of the process, glimpses of gnosis that deepen the practitioner's connection with their own inner truth. In these moments, the soul perceives itself more clearly, as if a fog lifts, revealing the path ahead.

The ultimate aim of Gnostic self-analysis is not merely self-understanding but transformation. Through consistent observation, self-questioning, and detachment, the seeker begins to release the layers of identity that obscure their true self. The habitual thoughts, emotions, and beliefs that once held sway gradually lose their grip, replaced by a clearer, purer awareness. The self that emerges is not defined by the ego's needs or fears but by an inner wisdom that reflects the divine spark, unburdened by the limitations of the constructed self.

Each session of self-analysis strengthens the seeker's capacity for awareness, creating a firm foundation for the deeper Gnostic practices to come. The daily ritual of reflection, observation, and journaling builds a discipline of self-honesty, cultivating a relationship with the self that is both compassionate and discerning. Through this foundation, the practitioner prepares to encounter even greater mysteries on the Gnostic path, developing the resilience and clarity needed to walk the path with courage and openness.

In time, the seeker will see the fruits of this labor, noticing a profound shift in their experience of themselves and the world. The shadows that once seemed intimidating are seen with compassion, and the habitual patterns lose their power, replaced by an inner stillness that reflects the true self. With each step, the Gnostic practitioner draws closer to gnosis, the true knowledge that transcends intellect and reveals the radiant presence of the divine within.

As the seeker advances deeper into the practice of self-analysis, the journey becomes more intimate and profound, revealing subtler layers of consciousness and inviting an even more transformative level of inner work. Where earlier practices focused on observing and recognizing patterns, this stage guides the seeker toward integration, using advanced methods that reveal the hidden roots of behaviors, beliefs, and emotions, allowing for a fuller understanding of the self.

At the heart of this advanced self-analysis lies introspective journaling, an expansion of the basic journaling introduced in the first part. Now, the seeker moves beyond simply recording thoughts or events, delving into the why and how of their reactions, the origin of their feelings, and the unconscious motivations behind their actions. Introspective journaling is a tool of precision: it brings to light the shadows of the psyche, the buried memories, and subtle impressions that shape perception and reaction. By asking probing questions like, "What fears are hidden within this reaction?" or "What inner conflict does this pattern reflect?" the practitioner uncovers layers of self previously concealed.

The act of writing becomes an alchemical process, one that takes the seeker through a labyrinth of thoughts, revealing insights as they unfold on the page. Patterns that once seemed immutable—cycles of self-doubt, frustration, or resentment—begin to dissolve in the light of awareness. The seeker learns to examine each pattern with detachment, neither indulging in it nor suppressing it, but allowing it to reveal itself fully before gently releasing its hold. Over time, this process helps to transform ingrained habits, freeing the mind from old conditioning and creating space for new, conscious responses.

One of the most potent tools in this phase is dream analysis, a method that opens the doorway to the subconscious mind, where hidden aspects of the self often appear in symbolic form. Gnostic tradition has long revered dreams as a bridge between the material and spiritual worlds, a place where the soul communicates through symbols and stories. In this practice, the seeker learns to recall and interpret their dreams, recording them with care upon waking and reflecting on their symbols and meanings. Each figure, action, and setting in a dream is seen as a message, an image that represents aspects of the inner world, unfiltered by the rational mind.

The seeker might encounter recurring dream symbols—a certain place, figure, or action—that hold clues to unresolved inner conflicts or unrecognized desires. For example, dreams of being pursued may reflect fears or anxieties the conscious mind is reluctant to confront, while dreams of flying might represent a longing for freedom from limitations. As the practitioner analyzes these symbols, they develop a deeper understanding of the forces that shape their inner landscape. This process, guided by intuition, encourages the seeker to look beyond literal interpretations and explore the personal, often spiritual significance of each dream.

The practice of dream analysis is especially potent when coupled with intentional dreaming, a technique where the seeker sets a conscious intention before sleep, asking for guidance or insight into a particular issue. This request invites the subconscious mind to respond, often revealing answers through symbolic images or vivid scenarios. Intentional dreaming can lead to powerful breakthroughs, allowing the practitioner to receive wisdom from their own inner depths and guiding them toward greater self-awareness.

Alongside dream analysis, the Gnostic practitioner embraces deep reflection—a focused meditation practice that allows for extended contemplation on specific aspects of the self. This differs from general meditation, as it centers on a particular question or emotion, inviting the seeker to sit with it fully. During this practice, the practitioner might ask, "What unfulfilled desires linger within me?" or "How does anger arise, and what does it reveal?" By holding the question without seeking an immediate answer, the mind enters a receptive state, allowing insights to arise naturally, revealing layers of consciousness beyond immediate awareness.

This deep reflection leads to a process known as facing internal resistances. The seeker confronts the parts of themselves that resist change, growth, or vulnerability—the defense mechanisms that protect the ego from perceived threats. These resistances are subtle and often deeply ingrained, manifesting as stubborn habits, dismissive thoughts, or emotional reactions that arise without warning. By observing these resistances with patience, the practitioner can begin to understand their origins and release their hold. Each resistance is a doorway, an opportunity to uncover a part of the psyche that has been shaped by fear, insecurity, or attachment, revealing areas that require healing and compassion.

In this phase, the work of integration becomes paramount. As the practitioner brings hidden aspects of self into awareness, the next step is to accept and integrate them rather than reject or judge. Gnostic self-analysis teaches that every part of the self, no matter how uncomfortable, holds value and meaning. By embracing these parts with compassion, the seeker fosters a sense of wholeness, transcending dualistic views of "good" and "bad" within the self. This integration leads to a profound inner harmony, where each part of the psyche is acknowledged and aligned with the soul's true purpose.

A practice that aids in integration is active imagination, a form of meditative visualization in which the practitioner engages with different aspects of the self as though they were characters or figures in a story. For instance, an emotion like anger might be visualized as a figure, a symbol that the practitioner can dialogue with, asking questions and listening to its responses. In this way, active imagination allows the seeker to explore their inner world dynamically, understanding emotions as parts of themselves rather than as external forces. Each figure becomes a teacher, revealing lessons that bring the seeker closer to inner balance.

As the practitioner progresses through these techniques, they experience a gradual transformation in how they perceive themselves and their place in the world. The insights gained from introspective journaling, dream analysis, deep reflection, and active imagination lead to a shift in identity, from a self shaped by habits and reactions to one informed by inner wisdom and self-awareness. Old patterns begin to dissolve, replaced by a sense of agency and a clear vision of the self's potential. The seeker is no longer ruled by the shadows of the subconscious but instead moves with a quiet confidence, an understanding that they are more than the sum of their thoughts and emotions.

In this phase, the practitioner learns the art of integrating insights, translating them into daily life. Each realization, each breakthrough in self-understanding, becomes a guide for how they think, act, and relate to others. Integration means not only knowing oneself but acting from that knowledge, allowing inner truths to shape one's choices and behaviors. This alignment between inner and outer life is a hallmark of Gnostic self-transformation, where every action reflects the soul's wisdom, free from the constraints of past conditioning.

The advanced practices of Gnostic self-analysis offer a path to genuine personal transformation. By continuously facing the hidden layers of self with courage and compassion, the seeker transcends limitations, releasing attachments and fears that once held them back. They become attuned to the silent wisdom within, which leads them closer to gnosis—a state of being where the self is fully realized, balanced, and aligned with the divine.

Through this journey of self-discovery, the seeker cultivates an enduring inner peace and clarity. Each layer of understanding brings them nearer to the inner light that has always been present, waiting to be unveiled. This clarity is a treasure of the Gnostic path, a gift that transcends intellect and logic, grounding the practitioner in a profound truth that will guide them on the path ahead.

Chapter 5
Protection Rituals

Protection is a sacred act in the Gnostic journey, an intentional setting of boundaries between the inner sanctum of the self and the complex energies that populate the external world. This chapter introduces essential practices for creating spiritual protection, allowing the seeker to explore higher realms with confidence and safety. For the Gnostic practitioner, these rituals are not just symbolic gestures; they are powerful tools that shield the soul from influences that could cloud or distort the purity of inner experience.

The cornerstone of protection in Gnostic practice begins with visualization of light. This ritual serves as a foundational act, one that creates an energetic shield through the power of focused intention and imagery. The practitioner starts by sitting in a comfortable, meditative posture, closing their eyes and drawing their awareness inward. With each breath, they visualize a gentle, luminous light gathering within their heart center, a warm and radiant energy that represents divine protection. As this light grows brighter, the practitioner imagines it expanding outward, forming a sphere around their entire body.

This light becomes a protective barrier, repelling anything that does not serve the seeker's highest good. Each inhalation strengthens the light, each exhalation spreads it outward, until it envelops the practitioner like an unbreakable shield. This practice can be done at the start of meditation, before entering sacred spaces, or whenever the practitioner feels the need for extra protection. The visualization of light not only protects but also reinforces a connection with the divine essence, a reminder that the inner spark is a source of unyielding strength and guidance.

Following the practice of light visualization, the seeker is introduced to the concept of creating an energy shield. Unlike the softer visualization of light, this technique calls for a focused concentration on forming an armor-like barrier, a structure that is imagined as strong and resilient. The energy shield may be visualized as a wall of light, a reflective surface, or even as an ethereal cloak that surrounds the body. Some practitioners imagine it as an impenetrable field, one that reflects back any negative or intrusive energies, allowing only supportive and positive influences to enter. This shield, strengthened by focused intent, becomes a tool of both physical and spiritual security.

Protective symbols are another powerful element in the Gnostic toolkit. Throughout spiritual traditions, symbols have carried sacred meanings and energies, capable of invoking protection, strength, and guidance. The Gnostic practitioner may choose symbols that resonate with them personally, perhaps a cross, a pentagram, or another ancient emblem known for its protective qualities. Holding the symbol in mind or even drawing it physically on paper, the practitioner consecrates it through intention, infusing it with a specific purpose. For some, carrying an object etched with this symbol, such as a pendant or stone, serves as a tangible reminder of protection throughout the day.

The use of these symbols can also be incorporated into the light visualization and energy shield practices, reinforcing the layers of protection around the seeker. For instance, a practitioner might visualize the chosen symbol within the heart of their protective sphere or imagine it glowing at the boundary of their energy shield. These symbols, strengthened by the practitioner's intention and belief, become potent allies in the Gnostic path, keeping the practitioner attuned to the divine while filtering out distractions or disruptions.

Preparation of body and mind is equally important for protection rituals, as it allows the practitioner to enter these practices with clarity and focus. In Gnosticism, the preparation ritual often includes a cleansing of the body, which might involve washing hands or face as a symbolic act of purification. With each splash of water, the practitioner visualizes all external influences washing away, preparing the body to serve as a pure vessel for the spirit. This physical purification mirrors the deeper intention of spiritual clarity, setting the stage for focused and undistracted meditation or ritual.

Protective mantras further amplify the protective energies cultivated in these rituals. Gnostic traditions often include sacred phrases or sounds—mantras designed to create vibrations that resonate with protection. The seeker may choose a word or phrase that feels empowering, repeating it quietly or silently. Some find resonance with ancient Gnostic invocations, such as the mantra "Sophia" to invoke divine wisdom and guidance, or "Pleroma" to connect with the fullness of divine protection. As the mantra is repeated, the seeker feels a shift in energy, as though surrounded by an invisible barrier woven from sound and intent, reinforcing the power of the ritual.

In a group setting, these protection practices can take on an even greater strength. When performed with others, the combined energy creates a collective field of protection that enhances each individual's shield. In group rituals, the participants may hold hands or stand in a circle, envisioning a shared sphere of light that encompasses all within it. Together, they chant a chosen mantra or hold a symbol collectively, their intentions aligning as one. This collective intention magnifies the effects of protection, creating a safe space for communal practice and shared spiritual exploration.

For those who work alone, protection rituals remain equally potent, as each practitioner's personal connection with the divine serves as the ultimate source of protection. Over time, as the seeker integrates these practices into daily life, the sense of protection becomes second nature, a subtle but ever-present awareness of safety and clarity. The light shield, energy armor, and mantras become tools that are as natural to call upon as breathing, always available, creating a constant sense of sanctuary regardless of the surrounding environment.

Protection is not merely a safeguard against external forces; it is a cultivation of inner strength. The more the practitioner engages with these rituals, the more they strengthen their own inner resolve, finding that true protection arises from within. The light shield and energy barrier become reflections of an inner clarity and purity that naturally guard against distraction or negativity. This clarity enables the practitioner to approach each Gnostic practice without fear, rooted in the certainty that their connection to the divine provides all the security they need.

As the seeker becomes attuned to the energies that surround and interact with them, they may find that protection rituals extend into ordinary life. Each moment, each encounter, is experienced with a sense of presence and awareness, allowing them to discern which influences to welcome and which to avoid. The rituals serve not only as protection for the soul but as a reminder that the practitioner's true nature is invulnerable, connected to an essence that transcends all temporal forces.

With these foundational practices, the Gnostic practitioner is well-prepared for the deeper explorations to come. These protection rituals form a vital layer in the spiritual journey, enabling the seeker to walk the path with confidence and openness. With each visualization, symbol, and mantra, the practitioner reinforces their commitment to self-knowledge and spiritual integrity, cultivating a sacred space within and around themselves that preserves the purity of their journey. In this safe, protected space, the soul may rise to meet the divine unencumbered, ready to receive the mysteries that await.

In the deepening of Gnostic protection rituals, the practitioner learns to craft and consecrate objects of power—talismans and amulets imbued with protective intent. These artifacts serve as physical manifestations of inner strength and spiritual focus, anchoring the divine energies cultivated within the practitioner's rituals. Crafted with deliberate intention, talismans and amulets transform into personal symbols of protection, grounding the practitioner's spiritual focus and providing continuous shielding from unwanted influences.

The creation of a talisman begins with an object carefully chosen to resonate with the seeker's intentions, such as a stone, pendant, or small figurine. Each element of the talisman's composition should hold meaning, perhaps selected for its natural properties or symbolic value. Crystals like black tourmaline or amethyst are traditionally used for their grounding and protective qualities, while metals like silver can enhance purity and clarity. The practitioner cleanses the object with water, smoke, or intention, preparing it as a blank slate for the energies that will be instilled.

Once cleansed, the object is consecrated in a ritual designed to link it with the divine. This consecration involves focusing intent upon the object, visualizing it filled with light, and invoking specific energies for protection. The practitioner might hold the object in their hands, breathing slowly and visualizing protective light filling it from all sides. They may whisper words of blessing, such as "May this talisman protect me and keep my path clear," or "Let this object be a shield against all that seeks to disrupt my harmony." Each word strengthens the talisman's connection to the practitioner's inner power and spiritual purpose.

In addition to talismans, the use of amulets brings further layers of protection, often bearing symbols or inscriptions that align with the Gnostic path. An amulet might be engraved with ancient symbols, such as the serpent to represent wisdom or the eye to symbolize divine vision. Carving or drawing these symbols onto an amulet infuses it with a specific protective energy, linking it to the seeker's path and intention. The practitioner then wears or carries the amulet, allowing it to act as an energetic shield that moves with them, subtly reinforcing their spiritual boundaries.

For those who wish to enhance the power of these objects, the use of specific plants and incense becomes an integral part of the ritual. Plants like sage, frankincense, and myrrh are known for their cleansing and protective properties, their smoke serving as a tangible barrier that clears and consecrates spaces and objects alike. The practitioner may light incense or burn these sacred herbs during the consecration ritual, allowing the smoke to envelop the talisman or amulet. This smoke, imbued with ancient and sacred qualities, carries away any lingering impurities, leaving the object ready to receive the protective energies of the divine.

Incense itself can be used to cleanse the practitioner's immediate space, enveloping the room in a layer of purification. Before beginning a meditation or ritual, the practitioner might light frankincense, allowing its fragrant smoke to fill the space and create an atmosphere of sanctity and protection. The practitioner stands within the smoke, visualizing it as a barrier that shields and purifies. This layer of smoke not only cleanses but also heightens the practitioner's spiritual sensitivity, sharpening their awareness and preparing them for profound inner work.

Beyond personal artifacts, group rituals for protection add another dimension of strength to the practice, reinforcing individual shields through collective intention. In such settings, each practitioner brings their own talisman or amulet, and together they perform a consecration ritual that binds each object to the shared energy of the group. Participants form a circle, holding their objects or focusing on a collective symbol, such as a sacred flame or a large crystal at the center. They might chant a protective mantra together, such as "Pleroma" or "Sophia," building a resonance that amplifies the shield around each member.

The group's combined energy creates a field of protection that is exponentially stronger than any single practitioner's. This group dynamic reinforces each individual's intentions, creating a shield that protects not only from external disturbances but also from inner fears or doubts that might arise during deep spiritual work. Each participant's object is charged by the collective energy, and upon leaving, they carry a tangible reminder of the protection and unity experienced in the ritual.

When working alone, the practitioner can also increase the potency of their protection by setting up a designated altar for protection. This altar is arranged with specific items and symbols that resonate with safety, strength, and divine guidance. A candle may be placed at its center, representing the flame of inner truth, surrounded by symbols such as a small mirror to reflect away negativity or crystals known for their protective properties. Each item is carefully chosen to support the intention of the altar, and the practitioner visits this space regularly to reinforce their sense of sanctuary.

Over time, the altar itself becomes an anchor, an energetic focal point where the practitioner can return to renew their sense of safety and grounding. Visiting the altar, lighting the candle, and spending a few quiet moments in its presence help reinforce the protective boundaries established through the ritual. This sacred space becomes a source of strength and stability, a reminder that the divine is both within and surrounding the practitioner, offering guidance and shielding from harm.

These protective practices expand beyond the ritual space, weaving themselves into the practitioner's life. With experience, the Gnostic seeker finds that the act of creating boundaries, both physical and spiritual, fosters a natural resilience and inner calm. The objects, symbols, and mantras become more than tools; they become extensions of the practitioner's will, reflections of the divine power within that knows how to protect and guide.

In moments of challenge or uncertainty, the practitioner need only touch their talisman, whisper a mantra, or visualize the light shield to reinforce their protection. These small acts serve as reminders that protection is always accessible, that divine support is ever-present, and that the Gnostic path offers not just insight but also strength.

The layers of protection cultivated through these rituals empower the practitioner to enter higher states of consciousness with assurance, free from the disruptions of uninvited energies. With the sacred shield in place, the practitioner approaches the

Gnostic mysteries with openness and calm, knowing that they are fully guarded by both inner strength and divine light.

The path forward is now illuminated and secure, a testament to the profound interplay between the human will and the divine, each reinforcing the other in the sacred dance of protection and revelation. With each ritual, each consecrated object, and each layer of smoke, the practitioner draws closer to the divine essence, shielded and prepared for the mysteries that await.

Chapter 6
Chakra Alignment

In the journey toward spiritual clarity, aligning the inner energies becomes an essential step, and within the Gnostic framework, this alignment finds particular importance. Chakras—centers of energy within the body—are understood as gateways between the material and spiritual worlds, influencing not only physical vitality but also mental clarity, emotional balance, and spiritual receptivity. For the Gnostic seeker, harmonizing these centers allows for a clearer connection with the divine spark within, facilitating insights, deepening meditative experiences, and supporting the work of inner transformation.

Chakras are often imagined as wheels or spirals of energy, each corresponding to specific physical, emotional, and spiritual aspects of life. In the Gnostic path, this alignment is not merely about balance but about aligning oneself with the inner light of gnosis, allowing each chakra to resonate with its fullest potential and serve as a channel for divine wisdom. The first step in this process is learning to recognize each energy center within the body, understanding its qualities, and identifying any blockages or imbalances that may hinder spiritual development.

The practice begins at the root chakra, located at the base of the spine. This center represents our foundation, anchoring us to the material world, embodying survival, stability, and a sense of belonging. For the Gnostic practitioner, grounding at the root chakra ensures that they are firmly planted, both physically and energetically, a foundation from which the journey of self-knowledge can safely unfold. The seeker may visualize a red, glowing light at the base of the spine, radiating warmth and strength, envisioning it as a root connecting deep into the earth. This grounding visualization serves to clear any fear or instability, allowing the practitioner to feel supported, rooted in a secure base.

The next center, the sacral chakra, located just below the navel, holds the energy of creation, desire, and emotional flow. Within Gnosticism, this center represents the balance of creative forces, both within oneself and with the world. The seeker visualizes a warm orange light, expanding gently through the lower abdomen, and imagines it as a steady flame that illuminates their capacity for joy, intimacy, and creative expression. By aligning the sacral chakra, the practitioner cultivates a sense of emotional fluidity, allowing feelings to arise and pass without attachment or suppression.

Moving upward, the solar plexus chakra, located just above the navel, resonates with willpower, confidence, and personal power. Here, the seeker encounters the energy that fuels determination and self-awareness. In Gnostic practice, the solar plexus is a point of inner strength, a place from which the practitioner exerts their will toward spiritual progress. Visualizing a vibrant yellow light radiating from this center, the seeker feels warmth spreading through the abdomen, as though a golden sun were glowing within. This light strengthens the practitioner's sense of purpose, illuminating a path of discipline and courage.

At the heart of the journey lies the heart chakra, the center of love, compassion, and divine connection. In Gnostic understanding, this chakra represents the bridge between the earthly and the divine, a place where the soul feels the whisper of the inner light. The seeker envisions a green light in the center of the chest, expanding with each breath, filling the heart with an unconditional warmth that softens judgment and opens the way to inner harmony. Here, the practitioner experiences the first inklings of divine love, a sense of connection that goes beyond self, embracing others and the cosmos itself. This openness is crucial for Gnostic work, as it enables the seeker to approach the mysteries with humility and an open heart.

The throat chakra, located at the center of the neck, is next. It governs expression, truth, and communication, making it vital for the Gnostic's exploration of inner truth. Visualizing a blue light, the seeker imagines this chakra expanding, clearing any obstacles that prevent authentic expression. In the Gnostic context, the throat chakra is not just about speaking; it is about expressing one's divine nature, aligning words and actions with inner truths. This alignment fosters honesty, integrity, and clarity, supporting the seeker's ability to articulate insights gained along the path.

Rising higher, the third eye chakra, situated between the eyebrows, is a focal point for intuition, insight, and inner vision. For the Gnostic practitioner, this chakra represents the faculty of spiritual perception, an inner sight that goes beyond ordinary understanding. By focusing on a violet or indigo light, the seeker cultivates a connection with this inner vision, allowing the light to radiate through the mind, dissolving illusions and expanding awareness. This center, when aligned, becomes a doorway to gnosis, where insights arise not from logic but from direct experience, revealing truths that transform perception.

Finally, the journey ascends to the crown chakra, positioned at the top of the head, representing connection to the divine, unity, and pure consciousness. In the Gnostic tradition, this center is seen as the culmination of all spiritual work, the point where the soul reconnects with the Pleroma, the realm of divine fullness. Visualizing a radiant white or violet light at the crown, the practitioner allows this light to open like a lotus flower, connecting upward to the infinite source of divine wisdom. The crown chakra represents a state of transcendence, a space where the self merges with the universal, experiencing a glimpse of divine oneness.

In each meditation session, the practitioner visits these centers sequentially, taking time to visualize, breathe into, and clear each one. By engaging each chakra, the seeker tunes each center to resonate with their highest purpose, removing any imbalances or blockages that may cloud perception. This sequential approach encourages an energetic flow that moves upward through the body, awakening the practitioner's innate sensitivity to the divine energies within.

Beyond simple visualization, the seeker can employ breathwork to assist in the alignment process. By breathing deeply into each chakra, focusing on expanding and contracting the energy center with each breath, the practitioner activates and cleanses these vital points. This breath-focused practice brings the seeker's awareness directly into each center, facilitating an embodied connection that anchors spiritual insights within the physical self. Each breath becomes an act of devotion, a means of aligning the body and soul with the highest aspirations of the Gnostic path.

As the practitioner engages in regular chakra alignment, they begin to experience shifts in their inner landscape—emotions become more balanced, thoughts clearer, and their sense of purpose more focused. Aligning the chakras helps dissolve the emotional and energetic blockages that obscure the path of gnosis, fostering a state of inner harmony that is both grounding and expansive. Each aligned chakra contributes to a holistic state of openness, where the body, mind, and soul work in unison, enhancing the practitioner's receptivity to spiritual insights.

This alignment serves as a foundation for deeper practices on the Gnostic path, creating a vessel that is finely tuned to receive and reflect the divine light within. As each energy center vibrates with balance and clarity, the practitioner becomes a mirror for the divine, grounded in the material yet open to the realms beyond. Each step in the alignment process is a step toward unity, preparing the practitioner for the profound spiritual revelations that await, ready to welcome the sacred into every part of their being.

With the basics of chakra alignment established, the Gnostic practitioner now explores a deeper engagement with each energy center, delving into advanced methods of cleansing, activation, and harmonization. This journey through the chakras becomes a sacred ritual, where each center is seen not merely as an energy hub but as a spiritual gateway. These advanced practices help the seeker cultivate a refined awareness, where each chakra's unique qualities are brought into resonance with the whole being, creating a harmonic field that amplifies the soul's connection to the divine.

The process begins with focused meditations on individual chakras, dedicating concentrated attention to each center, moving beyond basic visualization and into a dynamic relationship with the energy it holds. Each meditation allows the practitioner to dive deeper into the specific qualities and energies of the chakra, exploring its role and influence on the mind, body, and spirit. By focusing on the root chakra, for instance, the practitioner delves into the concept of grounding, stability, and safety, examining how their connection to the material world influences their spiritual journey. Visualizing roots extending from the base of the spine, grounding the practitioner in the earth, this meditation cultivates a deep inner calm and strengthens the foundation from which all other spiritual work can unfold.

The advanced chakra practice then shifts to energy cleansing techniques, where each center is purified of stagnant or unhelpful energies that may have accumulated over time. Practitioners can use tools like crystals or herbal incense, selecting items that resonate with each chakra's specific vibration. For example, red jasper or garnet may be used to purify and empower the root chakra, while amethyst serves to cleanse the crown chakra. The seeker holds the crystal or wafts the incense near each chakra, visualizing any dark or heavy energy being lifted away, replaced by a vibrant, clear light. This practice not only removes blockages but also energizes each center, bringing a renewed vitality to the practitioner's energy body.

Sound healing becomes another profound technique for chakra alignment, using resonant frequencies to bring each chakra into its optimal state. Each chakra corresponds to a specific frequency, and chanting or listening to particular tones or mantras can activate and harmonize them. For example, the sound "LAM" is chanted to activate the root chakra, while "OM" is used for the crown. By chanting these sounds or listening to them in a meditative state, the practitioner tunes each energy center, aligning their vibrational frequency with the highest aspects of their being. The vibrations created by sound penetrate deeply, dislodging hidden blockages and encouraging the natural flow of energy throughout the chakra system.

To amplify the connection with each energy center, the practitioner employs guided visualizations tailored to the Gnostic path. Each chakra is seen as a portal that offers access to specific insights or spiritual qualities. For instance, when meditating on the heart chakra, the practitioner may envision a green, glowing lotus opening petal by petal, releasing waves of compassion and love that radiate throughout their body and beyond. This visualization deepens the experience of love and empathy, transforming these qualities into spiritual strengths that guide interactions with others and align the practitioner's life with the essence of Gnostic teachings.

As the practitioner progresses, they explore the concept of balancing dual energies within the chakras. This balancing act, inspired by the dualistic nature of Gnosticism, acknowledges that each chakra holds a dynamic tension between opposing qualities—strength and gentleness, stability and flexibility, willpower and surrender. By meditating on these dual aspects within each chakra, the seeker learns to cultivate balance, allowing each energy center to express itself harmoniously. For example, the sacral chakra, linked with emotions and creativity, holds the balance between attachment and release. Meditating on this chakra with awareness of this duality fosters a healthy emotional life, where feelings are experienced fully yet without attachment, allowing creativity to flow unimpeded.

For deeper integration, the practitioner is introduced to the chakra breathing technique, a practice of conscious breathing that moves energy through the chakra system in a flowing rhythm. In this technique, the seeker begins with a deep breath into the root chakra, filling it with energy, then moves the breath upward to the sacral, solar plexus, and so on, until it reaches the crown. On the exhale, the breath descends, moving from the crown back to the root, creating a circuit of energy that circulates throughout the body. This rhythmic breathing harmonizes the chakras, allowing energy to move freely up and down the spine, enhancing vitality and creating a sense of unity within the self. Practicing this cyclic breathing strengthens the connection between mind and body, fostering a sense of wholeness that is essential for spiritual clarity.

The seeker is encouraged to integrate color therapy in their advanced chakra practice, using colored fabrics, lighting, or visualizations that correspond to each chakra's unique hue. During meditation, the practitioner may place a cloth of the chakra's color nearby or imagine being bathed in that color's light, allowing it to permeate the energy center fully. Each color activates and harmonizes specific frequencies within the chakra, enhancing its qualities. Red for the root, orange for the sacral, yellow for the solar plexus, green for the heart, blue for the throat, indigo for the third eye, and violet or white for the crown. This use of color adds a subtle but powerful dimension to the chakra practice, engaging the subconscious and reinforcing the energetic effects.

As each chakra is aligned and cleansed, the practitioner experiences an energetic balance that opens the door to higher states of consciousness. In this state, the seeker finds that thoughts are clearer, emotions more balanced, and perceptions more profound. The aligned chakras form a bridge, connecting the earthly self with the higher realms of the soul, allowing the practitioner to move through life with a heightened sense of awareness and purpose. Each aligned chakra contributes to an overall sense of peace and clarity, creating a channel through which the divine spark can radiate without obstruction.

Regular practice of these advanced techniques begins to transform not only the practitioner's inner world but also their experience of the external world. Relationships, interactions, and even challenges are approached with a calm and balanced energy.

The harmonized chakras enable the practitioner to remain rooted yet open, expressive yet reflective, confident yet humble. This integration of spiritual qualities strengthens the seeker's presence, allowing them to act from a place of authenticity and deep inner connection.

Ultimately, advanced chakra alignment aligns the practitioner with the Gnostic ideal of inner knowledge and divine union. Each chakra becomes a point of illumination, a star in the constellation of the soul, through which the light of gnosis shines. This alignment is not simply a state of personal peace but a preparation for deeper spiritual work, where the soul is able to ascend through layers of consciousness, touching realms of insight and wisdom that reveal the nature of the divine.

In this expanded state, the chakras act as conduits for the higher self, harmonizing earthly experiences with spiritual realities. The journey through the chakras becomes a continuous practice, each session reinforcing the unity between body and spirit, between self and cosmos. Through the process of alignment, the seeker establishes a sacred sanctuary within, a place of stillness and radiance where the divine essence speaks in the language of light, guiding each step on the Gnostic path.

Chapter 7
Initiation Rituals

In the world of Gnostic practice, initiation is not simply a rite of passage but an awakening—a conscious and deliberate step toward self-knowledge, where the practitioner encounters the sacred within. An initiation ritual marks the beginning of a profound journey, opening the door to a realm where the ordinary and divine meet. This chapter introduces the concept of Gnostic initiation, exploring the symbolic elements and ritual steps that bring the practitioner closer to their divine essence.

An initiation begins with an intention, set deeply in the heart of the seeker. This intention is more than a desire; it is a commitment to walk a path that will uncover layers of self, transcend ego, and connect with higher states of awareness. Before embarking on the ritual, the seeker reflects on this intention, contemplating questions such as "What am I seeking to understand about myself?" and "How do I wish to deepen my connection with the divine?" This quiet reflection serves to center the seeker, clarifying their purpose as they prepare to step into the unknown.

The setting for the initiation is created with care, turning an ordinary space into a sacred one. For Gnostic practitioners, this involves crafting an environment that resonates with the symbolic and spiritual energies of the ritual. Candles, representing the inner flame of wisdom, are often placed at the center of the space, their light a reminder of the divine spark that each soul carries. Crystals or stones—symbols of earth's grounding energy—are arranged around the space to establish balance, creating an atmosphere where the seeker feels both rooted and elevated.

Before the ritual begins, the practitioner undergoes a personal purification, symbolic of the readiness to cast off limitations and approach the divine with an open heart. This cleansing may involve washing hands or face, symbolizing the washing away of old patterns and inviting a fresh beginning. The ritual space itself is also purified; burning incense or smudging with sage clears any lingering energies, transforming the area into a sanctuary where only the highest intentions may enter.

The next stage of the initiation ritual involves invoking the sacred. The practitioner, standing in the center of the space, calls upon archetypal energies or figures from the Gnostic tradition that represent wisdom, protection, and guidance. Figures like Sophia, the embodiment of divine wisdom, or Logos, the principle of divine order, are envisioned as presences in the space, surrounding and supporting the seeker in their spiritual journey. Invocations may be spoken aloud or silently, depending on the practitioner's preference, each word carrying the weight of intention and commitment.

With the sacred energies invoked, the seeker is now prepared to engage with the symbolic elements of the ritual. One of the core symbols in Gnostic initiation is the circle, a representation of unity and protection. The practitioner may physically draw or imagine a circle around themselves, stepping into it as if crossing a threshold from the ordinary world into the divine realm. This circle signifies the boundary between the external and the internal, the temporal and the eternal, and within it, the practitioner stands poised between both worlds.

The act of lighting the central candle within this circle symbolizes the kindling of inner awareness, the awakening of the divine spark that has always been present but often hidden beneath layers of the mundane self. As the candle's flame flickers and steadies, the practitioner visualizes their own inner light beginning to glow, filling them with warmth and clarity. This flame is not just a symbol but a point of focus, a radiant reminder of the soul's journey toward wholeness and divine unity.

Another key element of the initiation is affirming intentions aloud. Speaking these words creates a powerful resonance, grounding the practitioner's purpose and transforming abstract intention into active commitment. For example, the practitioner might declare, "I seek to know myself truly, to walk a path of wisdom and light." These affirmations are a pledge to the self and the divine, an acknowledgment of the journey ahead with all its trials and revelations.

At the heart of the ritual lies a moment of silent communion with the divine essence within. With eyes closed and mind focused on the light within, the practitioner enters a state of quiet meditation, inviting the wisdom and presence of the inner self to arise. In this silence, the seeker might sense an expanding awareness, a feeling of unity with the universe, or a gentle but profound connection with the divine spark. This communion is a threshold experience, a taste of the deeper gnosis that lies at the heart of the Gnostic path.

To seal the initiation, the practitioner often engages in a gesture of grounding, such as placing hands upon the earth or touching the forehead in gratitude. This gesture brings the experience back into the physical realm, grounding the energies stirred during the ritual. By connecting with the earth or grounding through physical touch, the practitioner affirms that the wisdom gained during the initiation is not just ethereal but an integral part of their life journey.

The ritual concludes with a final blessing, a quiet expression of gratitude for the insights, protection, and guidance received. The practitioner may offer thanks to the invoked archetypal energies, honoring Sophia, Logos, or the Pleroma as sources of inspiration and support. This gratitude is a gesture of humility, a reminder that while the path of gnosis is deeply personal, it is also part of a larger, universal journey toward divine understanding.

After the initiation, the practitioner often takes time for quiet reflection, allowing the experience to settle and integrate within their consciousness. In the days following the ritual, they may experience subtle shifts in awareness, feeling more attuned to their inner world and more receptive to insights that arise from within. These shifts are the beginnings of gnosis, the lived knowledge that grows as the practitioner continues on the Gnostic path.

The initiation ritual thus serves as both a beginning and a transformation, a sacred act that marks the entry into a deeper phase of spiritual exploration. Through the symbolic elements, affirmations, and communion, the practitioner aligns themselves with a higher purpose, embracing the journey of self-discovery with openness and courage. The divine spark, once kindled, becomes a guiding light, illuminating the path ahead and empowering the seeker to uncover the mysteries that lie within.

Having established the foundation of initiation, the Gnostic seeker is now prepared to engage in more profound initiation rituals that draw upon complex symbols, invocations, and sacred archetypes. This deeper layer of initiation connects the practitioner with the core mysteries of Gnostic tradition, inviting them to explore realms of consciousness where inner and outer worlds converge. Here, the initiation transforms from an individual rite into an immersive, multi-dimensional experience, a profound communion with the divine forces that guide the Gnostic path.

At the heart of this advanced initiation lies the practice of sacred invocations, a call to the archetypal energies and deities that embody the wisdom and mysteries of Gnosticism. Unlike earlier stages where the practitioner may invoke only general qualities, these advanced rituals involve connecting with specific figures, such as Sophia—the embodiment of divine wisdom, or the Aeons, eternal beings that represent aspects of the Pleroma. Each invocation is a deliberate opening of the self to these energies, allowing them to inform and elevate the soul. The seeker begins by centering themselves in silence, then speaks each invocation slowly, with full presence, calling upon the figure with intention, respect, and receptivity.

The space for these rituals is arranged with heightened care, incorporating symbols and materials that resonate with the invoked archetypes. For a ritual invoking Sophia, for example, elements like a single white feather or a crystal prism might be placed on the altar, symbolizing purity, insight, and divine wisdom. Incense, herbs, and candles in colors that resonate with the archetype help to create an atmosphere that mirrors the energy of the invoked presence. Each object becomes more than a symbol; it is an extension of the archetype itself, a tangible bridge between the visible and the invisible.

The practitioner, within this sacred space, performs a rite of embodiment, an advanced technique of merging their consciousness with the archetype's essence. In the ritual invoking Sophia, the seeker envisions the divine wisdom descending as a gentle, radiant light, filling the body and mind, merging with their own spirit. This fusion allows the seeker to experience Sophia's qualities from within, dissolving the boundary between self and archetype. The initiation becomes an encounter, a temporary shift where the practitioner absorbs the archetype's wisdom, love, and clarity as if it were their own, experiencing divine qualities directly within their being.

These encounters are supported by specific chants or mantras associated with each archetype. For example, the mantra "Sophia" may be repeated softly, resonating in the seeker's mind and aligning their energy with the archetype. In advanced rituals, mantras are not only vocalized but allowed to sink into silence, resonating in the soul's depths. The practitioner allows the mantra to become a silent hum within, creating a vibrational field that aligns with the divine energy of the archetype. This silent chant serves as a bridge, allowing the seeker to enter a meditative state where the archetype's wisdom can be perceived more directly and intimately.

In some initiation rituals, the practitioner may perform a rite of symbolic offering, a gesture of humility and readiness to receive. This might involve placing an object of personal significance on the altar or creating a small, written reflection on what they are willing to release or transform. The offering is not material; it is an inner sacrifice, a symbolic release of an attachment, habit, or fear that limits spiritual growth. Through this offering, the practitioner expresses their openness to the archetype's guidance, signaling a willingness to be transformed.

At this stage, the ritual moves into a meditative phase of guided visualization, where the practitioner journeys through symbolic realms associated with the archetype. For example, in an initiation to connect with the Pleroma, the practitioner might visualize themselves in a vast, star-lit expanse—a boundless realm filled with glimmers of divine presence, where the infinite energies of the Aeons converge in perfect unity. Here, the seeker becomes both witness and participant in a profound experience of oneness, a momentary glimpse into the divine fullness that is the source of all being. The visualization is not simply an act of imagination but an experiential immersion, a moment where inner sight opens to truths beyond ordinary perception.

After this journey, the practitioner may experience a period of sacred silence, a quiet interval allowing the visions and experiences to settle. The silence is filled with meaning, a moment of stillness where the energies invoked and the insights received permeate the soul. In this silence, the practitioner attunes to subtleties within, sensing changes in awareness, clarity, or intuition. This silence is the soul's language, a space where insights from the ritual are absorbed and internalized, forming a foundation for future growth.

To conclude, the initiation ritual ends with a blessing and sealing of energies, a conscious act of grounding the experiences within the physical and spiritual body. The practitioner might touch the center of their chest or forehead, visualizing the divine energies descending from the crown to the heart, then down through the body to the earth. By anchoring these energies, the seeker ensures that the wisdom and insights gained from the ritual remain integrated, accessible as sources of strength and guidance on the Gnostic path.

The practitioner may feel subtle shifts in perception, intuition, or self-understanding following this advanced initiation. They may notice an expanded awareness of the archetypes and energies that influence their thoughts and actions, an alignment that brings a new level of spiritual clarity and connection to the divine. Over time, this initiatory experience deepens, shaping the seeker's journey and infusing their life with a sense of purpose and insight that extends far beyond the ritual space.

This complex initiation ritual is transformative, marking a significant step in the seeker's spiritual evolution. The practitioner becomes aware that they are not merely learning about the divine but are part of it, engaging directly with the archetypal forces that shape all aspects of existence. In this sacred space of initiation, the seeker has glimpsed their inner divinity and strengthened their connection to the sacred mysteries that define the Gnostic path.

With each step forward, each invocation and symbolic offering, the Gnostic practitioner moves deeper into the heart of spiritual understanding, prepared to meet the mysteries that lie ahead with wisdom, courage, and a profound sense of unity with the divine.

Chapter 8
Creative Visualization

Creative visualization in the Gnostic tradition serves as a profound tool for manifesting inner truths and aligning oneself with higher realities. In this practice, the mind becomes an instrument that transforms thoughts into vivid images, drawing upon the symbolic language of the unconscious to access realms beyond the material. For the Gnostic seeker, creative visualization is not just imagination; it is a purposeful act of engaging with the soul's inner wisdom, awakening archetypal energies that support spiritual evolution and self-discovery.

The foundation of creative visualization lies in understanding the mind's natural ability to shape perceptions and channel energies. The practice begins by quieting the mind through focused breathing, allowing the practitioner to enter a relaxed, open state, receptive to deeper imagery and symbolic insight. In this calm space, the seeker becomes the creator of an inner world, shaping images that resonate with their spiritual intentions. This focus on intention transforms visualization from passive dreaming into an active journey, where every image created serves a purpose and every detail holds meaning.

An initial exercise in Gnostic creative visualization involves imagining oneself as a vessel of divine light. The practitioner closes their eyes, breathing slowly and deeply, envisioning a warm, radiant light within the center of their chest. This light expands outward with each breath, filling the entire body, wrapping around every cell and gradually extending beyond, creating a luminous aura. This aura represents the divine spark within, a radiant presence that not only protects but also connects the practitioner to higher realms. By visualizing this light, the seeker experiences a subtle shift, a reminder of their true essence and their connection to the divine.

Next, the practitioner learns to work with personal symbols, selecting images that resonate with their spiritual journey. These symbols—such as a flame for inner knowledge, a star for guidance, or a serpent for transformation—are visualized in detail, allowing the mind to connect with the deeper meanings embedded within each one. The chosen symbol is not random; it represents an aspect of the self that the practitioner seeks to understand or cultivate. For instance, visualizing a flame encourages clarity and illumination, invoking the light of gnosis to guide the practitioner's steps.

To deepen this connection with symbols, the seeker visualizes holding the chosen symbol in their hands or surrounding themselves with its energy. For example, when working with the star as a symbol, the practitioner may imagine themselves standing under a night sky filled with stars, one particular star shining brightly and drawing their attention. This star, glowing with an intense but gentle light, becomes a guiding force, a reminder of the higher path and the soul's alignment with divine purpose. Through repetition, this visualization strengthens the connection between the seeker and the symbol, embedding it as a source of insight and resilience.

Nature-based visualizations are another powerful practice within creative visualization, allowing the practitioner to draw inspiration and strength from natural elements that reflect divine qualities. One effective exercise involves envisioning oneself as a tree, with roots extending deep into the earth, drawing nourishment and stability from the soil. The trunk represents the practitioner's strength and resilience, while the branches reach upward, embracing the light and connecting with the celestial. This visualization cultivates a sense of balance and groundedness, reminding the practitioner of their place within both the physical and spiritual realms.

Once comfortable with basic symbols and natural imagery, the practitioner is encouraged to explore visualizations of the inner temple, a sacred, personal space crafted entirely within the mind. This inner temple serves as a retreat, a sanctuary where the seeker can engage in reflection, meditation, and communion with the divine. The practitioner closes their eyes and envisions a space filled with symbols that hold personal meaning—a flame at the center, symbols of wisdom inscribed on the walls, a tranquil pool representing inner stillness. In this sacred space, the practitioner finds refuge, connecting deeply with the higher self and seeking guidance in moments of doubt or confusion.

To make this temple even more potent, the seeker might choose a single sacred object to be placed at its center—an object that represents a specific spiritual quality, such as a crystal for clarity, a rose for compassion, or a book for wisdom. Each time they enter the inner temple, the practitioner reconnects with this object, affirming its meaning and aligning with its essence. Over time, this object becomes a focal point of the temple, grounding the seeker in their spiritual path and reminding them of their highest aspirations.

Another transformative exercise within creative visualization is pathwork meditation, where the practitioner visualizes a journey through a symbolic landscape, each step revealing insights and deeper understanding. This journey might begin at the entrance to a forest, a path winding forward into an unknown landscape. As the practitioner walks along the path, they encounter symbols and images that hold personal meaning—perhaps a river representing emotions, a mountain symbolizing challenges, or a clearing that offers clarity and rest. Each element of the journey is encountered with openness and curiosity, interpreted intuitively by the practitioner as a message from the inner self.

During the pathwork, the practitioner may meet a figure—a wise guide, a reflection of the higher self, or an archetype from Gnostic tradition. This figure, whether human, animal, or even an ethereal presence, offers guidance and insight. In one exercise, the practitioner envisions encountering Sophia, the embodiment of divine wisdom, whose presence radiates peace and understanding. Sophia's guidance is received through imagery or words, often conveying a message that resonates deeply with the practitioner's current spiritual questions or challenges. This encounter is not merely an imaginative exercise but a direct communion with aspects of the soul, offering wisdom that transcends the intellect.

As the practitioner's skill in creative visualization grows, they learn to bring these inner images into daily life, using visualization to shape thoughts, actions, and responses. For instance, in moments of anxiety, the seeker might visualize the protective aura of light created during meditation, allowing it to calm and shield them from external disturbances. In challenging situations, the practitioner recalls the rooted stability of the tree visualization, grounding themselves in a sense of inner strength. Through these small, daily applications, the practice of visualization transforms from an isolated ritual into an integrated, living tool that guides and supports the practitioner on their path.

The practice of creative visualization cultivates an awareness of the power of intention and focus, awakening the Gnostic practitioner to the inner resources that shape their reality. By consistently engaging with symbols, creating sacred spaces, and journeying through inner landscapes, the seeker builds a bridge between their conscious self and the vast, symbolic language of the soul. Each image created, each journey undertaken, is a step toward a deeper understanding of the self, where imagination becomes a sacred tool for realizing the divine potential within.

This foundational work in creative visualization prepares the practitioner for even greater explorations of the mind and soul, a tool that not only supports spiritual growth but also embodies it. As the seeker learns to engage with the world through these inner images and symbols, they begin to see life itself as a reflection of the divine, a canvas upon which the sacred is continually revealed. In this practice, imagination is not a mere play of the mind but a powerful path to the heart of gnosis, where the soul's truth unfolds in images, symbols, and visions that transcend words.

Having laid the groundwork in the practice of creative visualization, the Gnostic practitioner now embarks on an advanced exploration of visualization techniques, engaging with archetypal images and symbols that hold transformative power. At this stage, creative visualization is no longer just an inward journey but an active engagement with the spiritual forces and archetypes that influence the inner and outer world. These advanced techniques deepen the practitioner's connection with the Gnostic path, offering insights that emerge not from thought alone but through the direct experience of the divine's symbolic language.

Central to this advanced practice is visualization with archetypal symbols—ancient images that carry layers of meaning and resonate with the spiritual core of humanity. These symbols, like the serpent, the key, and the lotus, are not chosen at random; each holds a specific significance, often found within Gnostic teachings and mystical traditions. The practitioner begins by selecting an archetypal symbol that resonates deeply with them, focusing on it in meditative silence, allowing its presence to expand within the mind's eye. This symbol becomes an anchor, a bridge to deeper layers of consciousness where its meanings reveal themselves.

One effective technique involves visualizing the chosen symbol not as static but as dynamic, shifting in form and revealing hidden aspects. For instance, the practitioner might visualize the serpent, an image found in many Gnostic texts symbolizing wisdom and transformation. The serpent may be envisioned coiled within the self, representing latent spiritual potential, or moving upward, symbolizing the rising of wisdom through the chakras or the energy channels within. As the practitioner watches the serpent move, it may reveal aspects of their own inner wisdom, resilience, or growth, embodying qualities that are ready to emerge.

Advanced visualization also introduces the use of elemental forces to enhance the power and depth of the practice. The seeker may visualize themselves in connection with the elements—earth, water, fire, air, and spirit—each element corresponding to specific aspects of spiritual growth and personal transformation. Earth offers grounding and stability, water represents emotional clarity and intuition, fire embodies the energy of transformation, air encourages mental clarity and insight, and spirit aligns with the divine essence. As the practitioner visualizes each element surrounding and interacting with their energy field, they attune to its qualities, allowing the elements to harmonize and purify their inner being.

For a deeper experience, the practitioner may visualize each element in sequence, allowing each one to infuse their body and mind. Earth is visualized as roots grounding them into the material world; water flows over and through them, cleansing emotions and memories; fire radiates warmth and burns away impurities; air brings fresh inspiration; and spirit surrounds them with divine light. By moving through these elements, the seeker harmonizes their inner energies, feeling a profound sense of unity with the natural and spiritual worlds.

As these visualizations become more refined, the practitioner explores ritualized visualization, a structured practice where symbols, elements, and archetypes are combined to create an intricate mental landscape. In ritualized visualization, the seeker may construct an inner scene, such as a sacred altar within a forest, where each element of the visualization has purpose and meaning. The forest may represent the unknown or inner depths, while the altar signifies a sacred space where transformation can occur. The practitioner places symbols on this altar that represent qualities they seek to embody or challenges they wish to overcome. For example, a chalice might symbolize the acceptance of wisdom, while a mirror could represent self-reflection and truth.

Within this imagined space, the practitioner performs symbolic acts, such as pouring water from the chalice over the altar, which represents a purification of the spirit, or gazing into the mirror to confront inner truths. Each action in the visualization serves as a catalyst for insight, creating a tangible, sensory experience that communicates directly with the unconscious. Through this ritualized visualization, the Gnostic practitioner brings the abstract into the concrete, engaging with inner truths in ways that words cannot capture.

Another transformative technique within advanced creative visualization is visualizing desired outcomes or personal transformation. Here, the seeker does not impose willful desires but visualizes themselves embodying qualities that align with their higher purpose and spiritual growth. If the practitioner seeks greater patience or compassion, they might visualize themselves in situations where these qualities naturally arise, feeling the calm patience or warm compassion extending from their heart to others. This practice is not about manifesting external goals but aligning inner qualities with the soul's higher calling, harmonizing desires with the divine essence.

Through this practice, the practitioner learns to envision challenges not as obstacles but as teachers, reflecting on the wisdom that each difficult experience offers. The seeker may visualize past experiences that caused pain or struggle, approaching them with the compassion and strength they have cultivated through visualization. By doing so, they transform the experience, dissolving emotional charges associated with it and integrating its lessons into their personal growth.

In a further extension of creative visualization, the practitioner learns to work with light as a transformative force. This involves visualizing a divine, radiant light filling and surrounding the body, representing purity, healing, and higher wisdom. The practitioner directs this light to specific areas in need of attention, such as the heart for emotional healing or the third eye for clarity and vision. This light becomes a source of continuous guidance, acting as both a shield and a revealer of insights, enabling the seeker to approach each aspect of their life with clarity and alignment.

In advanced creative visualization, the seeker also explores the use of Gnostic sigils, symbols specifically associated with divine or mystical meanings in Gnostic tradition. These sigils—formed from geometric shapes, letters, or images—are believed to hold powerful vibrations that resonate with particular spiritual qualities. The practitioner visualizes the chosen sigil glowing before them, imbued with energy, and allows its form to impress itself upon their consciousness. By focusing on the sigil, the practitioner aligns with the specific energy or intention it represents, be it protection, wisdom, or inner peace.

The final component of advanced creative visualization involves visualizing sacred landscapes, journeys into realms that represent stages of the soul's journey toward wholeness. The practitioner might visualize ascending a mountain, each step representing a personal challenge, or descending into a cave, symbolizing an exploration of the subconscious. At the summit or the cave's depth, the seeker encounters a vision or symbol that holds personal meaning, an answer to a question, or a message from the higher self. This journey, symbolic yet deeply personal, allows the practitioner to interact with aspects of the psyche and the divine that offer guidance and clarity.

As the practitioner completes these advanced visualizations, they bring the insights gained into their daily life, transforming thoughts and actions in ways aligned with their inner truths. Each visualization strengthens the connection between mind, spirit, and the divine, enhancing the practitioner's ability to approach life's challenges with wisdom and inner strength. By regularly engaging with these images and symbols, the practitioner develops a profound understanding of the self, the cosmos, and the divine forces that guide the Gnostic path.

Advanced creative visualization thus becomes a doorway, a sacred art that brings the practitioner closer to the mysteries within and beyond. Through symbols, light, elements, and sacred landscapes, the seeker discovers that the divine is always present, accessible through the imaginative language of the soul. This connection reveals life as an unfolding journey, where each moment and symbol becomes an invitation to know oneself and the divine in deeper, more meaningful ways.

Chapter 9
Spiritual Healing

The journey into Gnostic spiritual healing introduces the practitioner to methods that harness the inner divine for self-renewal, emotional balance, and the clearing of obstacles that obstruct the path of gnosis. Healing within Gnosticism is not solely the alleviation of pain or discomfort but a deeper reconciliation of the spirit, a return to the fullness of the soul's natural state. Through these practices, the seeker learns to tap into the divine essence within, awakening the energies that heal and transform, enabling the self to become a clearer vessel for higher consciousness.

The foundation of Gnostic spiritual healing begins with self-suggestion, a technique that aligns the conscious and subconscious mind toward harmony and healing. Self-suggestion involves using affirmations or declarations that instill confidence, peace, and balance within the practitioner. These affirmations may be simple, such as "I am whole and healed" or "I allow divine light to restore and renew me." By repeating these phrases with focused intent, the seeker initiates a process of gentle but profound change, as the subconscious mind aligns with the higher self, dissolving fears and inviting inner peace.

In the Gnostic context, these affirmations go beyond positive thinking; they are sacred decrees, infused with the divine energy that connects the practitioner to the Pleroma—the fullness of divine presence. The practitioner recites each affirmation slowly, breathing deeply with each repetition, allowing the words to resonate within their mind, heart, and spirit. This practice becomes a form of inner reprogramming, clearing the mind of limiting beliefs and instilling an awareness of divine potential and balance.

Another core technique in spiritual healing is energization, the practice of directing life force or divine energy through the body to activate healing and release blockages. The practitioner begins by sitting quietly, focusing on the breath, and visualizing a radiant white or golden light descending from above, entering through the crown of the head. This light, pure and vibrant, represents the healing energy of the divine. As the light fills the practitioner's body, it is directed to areas that feel tense, heavy, or blocked, often corresponding to places where energy has stagnated due to stress, unexpressed emotions, or unresolved experiences.

To deepen this process, the practitioner may place their hands on the area of the body where they feel the need for healing. This tactile connection creates a direct link between intent and physical presence, strengthening the flow of energy. With each breath, the practitioner visualizes this light radiating outward, dissolving any density, darkness, or discomfort, and restoring the body to a state of vibrant, flowing energy. This practice encourages the release of accumulated emotional burdens, opening space for renewal, and creating an overall sense of well-being.

In addition to energization, the seeker learns the practice of auric cleansing, a technique for purifying the subtle energy field that surrounds the body. The aura, often viewed as a luminous field of light, reflects the soul's current state and interacts with external energies. Throughout daily life, the aura can absorb residual energies from other people, environments, and experiences, which can lead to feelings of imbalance, confusion, or fatigue. Auric cleansing restores the purity of this field, allowing the soul's essence to shine without interference.

To perform an auric cleanse, the practitioner envisions a gentle rain of light descending from above, washing through the aura and carrying away any residual energy that does not belong.

The light flows through every layer of the aura, from the outer edges to the core closest to the body, revitalizing and restoring each level. The seeker may use visualization of color, imagining the aura bathed in bright, cleansing hues like white, gold, or violet. This process lifts away impurities and creates a sense of clarity, aligning the practitioner's energy field with the divine.

Breathwork also becomes an essential part of the Gnostic healing practice, as the breath is seen as a conduit for divine energy. Through controlled, rhythmic breathing, the practitioner channels vitality and clarity throughout the body, bringing balance to the mind and opening the spirit to higher states of awareness. One simple yet powerful technique involves deep diaphragmatic breathing, where the practitioner inhales deeply into the abdomen, holds the breath momentarily, and then exhales slowly. This rhythm of breath calms the nervous system, clears the mind, and creates a stable foundation for healing work.

With experience, the practitioner begins to apply specific patterns of breath, such as inhaling for a count of four, holding for a count of four, and exhaling for a count of four. Known as square breathing, this technique promotes inner balance, aligning the body and spirit in harmony. Through breathwork, the practitioner learns to control the flow of energy within, nurturing a sense of calm, reducing stress, and strengthening resilience to emotional fluctuations.

Another powerful aspect of Gnostic healing is sound resonance, the use of sound frequencies to stimulate healing and open channels within the energy body. Each sound or mantra has a particular vibration, resonating with specific energy centers or emotional states. For instance, the sound "OM" is chanted to create a unifying vibration, connecting the seeker with the universal consciousness. By softly chanting or listening to resonant sounds, the practitioner allows the frequencies to harmonize their energy field, dissolving stagnant energies and restoring the natural flow.

In the context of self-healing, the practitioner may choose a mantra that resonates with their intention for healing, perhaps chanting "HU," a Gnostic sound representing divine presence, or "AUM" for spiritual alignment. As the practitioner chants, the vibration permeates their being, creating a wave of energy that aligns the physical, mental, and spiritual layers of the self. Sound resonance becomes not only a tool for healing but also an invitation for divine energies to inhabit the practitioner's consciousness, bringing clarity and illumination.

Finally, the practitioner learns the practice of visualization healing, directing their inner vision to facilitate the body's natural healing processes. By visualizing a radiant light moving through the bloodstream or a gentle warmth surrounding tense muscles, the seeker aids the body's ability to repair and rejuvenate. This visualization is often accompanied by the feeling of gratitude, creating an environment of healing that is not driven by anxiety or need but by acceptance and compassion.

In one visualization, the practitioner may imagine the inner light traveling to an area of discomfort or imbalance, surrounding it with warmth and softness. As the light envelops this area, they may feel the tension dissolving, replaced by a sense of peace and relief. This process is repeated with patience and mindfulness, allowing the body and spirit to absorb the intention of healing and renewal.

Over time, these Gnostic healing practices transform the seeker's approach to health and well-being. They become attuned to their body's needs and energies, recognizing early signs of imbalance and addressing them before they manifest as physical discomfort. Healing evolves from a reactionary process to a proactive, daily practice that nourishes body, mind, and soul, fostering a state of continuous balance.

Gnostic spiritual healing is ultimately a journey toward self-integration, a recognition that true health arises from alignment with the divine. Through each technique—self-suggestion, energization, auric cleansing, breathwork, sound resonance, and visualization—the practitioner draws closer to the wholeness of their true self, experiencing health as a reflection of their inner harmony with the Pleroma.

As these techniques become integrated into the practitioner's life, healing is no longer seen as a mere response to discomfort but as a sacred practice that continually aligns the seeker with their highest potential, illuminating the path of gnosis with the light of a balanced and radiant spirit.

With foundational techniques of spiritual healing established, the Gnostic seeker now moves deeper into advanced methods that cultivate a heightened capacity for self-restoration and offer healing to others. This expanded approach to Gnostic healing introduces practices that address subtle and complex energies, guiding the practitioner in creating an atmosphere where negative energies dissolve and the soul's divine radiance can emerge fully. At this level, spiritual healing becomes not just a personal process but a transformative experience that extends outward, creating spaces of healing, alignment, and clarity.

One powerful tool at this stage is the ritual of clearing negative energies, a practice aimed at identifying and releasing dense or obstructive energies that accumulate in the physical, emotional, and spiritual fields. For this ritual, the practitioner begins by preparing a quiet space, lighting a candle to symbolize the light of the divine, and burning sacred herbs such as sage, palo santo, or frankincense, which are traditionally known for their purifying properties. As the smoke rises, the practitioner moves it around the body, from head to toe, envisioning the smoke carrying away any energy that does not serve their highest purpose.

During this ritual, the seeker may also use visualizations, imagining each breath releasing all lingering negative energy, replaced with a golden light that enters with each inhale. This light fills every corner of their being, dissolving shadows, softening tensions, and recharging the energy body. As this visualization unfolds, the practitioner experiences a renewal, a sense of inner clarity that leaves them feeling light, vibrant, and connected to the divine.

Following the cleansing ritual, the seeker can engage in aligning the spiritual body—a practice that balances and harmonizes the body's energetic layers. This alignment process involves lying or sitting comfortably, breathing deeply, and bringing awareness to each layer of the self: the physical body, emotional body, mental body, and spiritual body. Each layer is visualized as a distinct but interconnected field, vibrating in harmony and supporting one another. The practitioner may visualize a gentle current flowing from the earth to the crown of the head, energizing and balancing each layer as it ascends.

With each exhale, the practitioner releases any discordant energy, bringing the entire field into coherence and resonance with divine energy. As the seeker continues to practice alignment, they develop a natural sensitivity to imbalances in their spiritual body, becoming attuned to subtle shifts that may indicate a need for healing or realignment. This daily awareness allows the practitioner to maintain a steady state of inner harmony, reducing the accumulation of stress or tension in the spiritual field.

For those seeking to support others in their healing journey, remote healing offers a way to extend the gift of spiritual healing across distance, channeling energy and intention to support the well-being of another. This technique begins with grounding oneself and connecting with the divine essence within, creating a sacred space free of distractions. The practitioner then focuses on the individual receiving the healing, visualizing them surrounded by a soft, radiant light. This light is envisioned as a cocoon of energy that protects and nourishes, permeating every layer of their being.

In remote healing, the practitioner often uses a symbol of connection, such as visualizing a cord of light linking themselves with the person in need of healing. This connection is grounded in compassion and empathy, holding the intent that the recipient receives precisely what is needed for their highest good. As the practitioner holds this image, they may sense shifts in energy, as if the recipient's aura and energy field are being realigned and strengthened. By trusting the flow of divine energy, the practitioner allows the healing to occur naturally, refraining from imposing any specific outcome, and simply holding space for transformation.

An additional technique in advanced Gnostic healing is the use of mantras or sacred sounds to enhance and deepen the effects of healing. In this practice, the practitioner chants or intones specific sounds associated with divine qualities, such as "HU," representing the divine in Gnostic traditions, or "RA," for light and clarity. These sounds resonate with the body's energy centers, creating vibrations that dissolve stagnation and reinforce the soul's connection to the divine. By chanting these sounds during a healing session, the practitioner allows their voice to act as a conduit for the divine, harmonizing their own energies and extending this resonance to others.

As part of advanced healing, the practitioner also learns to create a healing altar—a physical and spiritual space dedicated to the continual alignment of energies. This altar might include objects with personal and spiritual significance, such as stones, crystals, candles, and sacred texts. Each item is selected with intention, creating a focal point for spiritual energies that support healing and alignment. The practitioner visits this altar regularly, spending a few moments in meditation, offering gratitude, and reaffirming their connection to the divine healing energies. This space serves as a sanctuary for the practitioner, a place where they can restore their energies and ground themselves before and after engaging in healing work.

Group healing practices offer a powerful experience, as multiple individuals come together with a shared intention of healing and transformation. In group settings, participants may form a circle, holding hands or creating a mental connection to strengthen the collective energy. Together, they visualize light or sound moving through each person, filling the circle with radiant energy that elevates and harmonizes. This group energy amplifies each individual's intentions, allowing a larger pool of healing energy to emerge. Group members often report feeling a powerful sense of unity, as if each soul were resonating with a single, divine note, reinforcing the bond between all present and aligning each person with a higher state of consciousness.

In cases where the practitioner is working to heal themselves from deeper emotional wounds or long-held blockages, they may engage in healing visualization journeys, where they visualize meeting a symbolic guide within themselves. This guide, often imagined as a compassionate figure like Sophia or a wise elder, represents the soul's inner wisdom. Through this guided visualization, the practitioner may encounter aspects of the self that are ready to be healed, areas where forgiveness, compassion, or understanding is needed.

The guide offers insights and comfort, serving as both healer and teacher. As the practitioner listens and receives these messages, they bring greater awareness to parts of themselves that may have been hidden or repressed. This inner healing journey becomes a path to self-compassion and self-reconciliation, where the practitioner learns to embrace the fullness of their own being, accepting both shadow and light.

Through these advanced healing practices, the Gnostic practitioner cultivates a capacity to heal not only themselves but also to contribute to the well-being of others and the world around them. Healing, in this light, is an extension of divine love and wisdom, a continuous alignment with the essence of gnosis, and an understanding of oneself as both healer and healed.

These techniques allow the practitioner to approach every aspect of life with a healing intention, to see every interaction and moment as an opportunity to cultivate balance, compassion, and harmony. Over time, healing becomes not merely an act but a way of being, an awareness that each soul's journey is a process of continual restoration, returning to the divine wholeness that underlies all existence.

This path of advanced spiritual healing thus transforms the Gnostic seeker, integrating body, mind, and spirit into a state of deep alignment. Each practice, each ritual, and each intention brings them closer to the essence of gnosis—where healing and wisdom flow from the same source, illuminating the seeker's path with the enduring light of the divine.

Chapter 10
The Path of Wisdom

The Gnostic journey is, at its core, a quest for wisdom—an understanding that transcends mere knowledge and penetrates the heart of truth itself. In Gnosticism, wisdom, often symbolized by Sophia, is the luminous guide that leads the seeker from the shadows of the material world into the fullness of spiritual reality. Embarking on the path of wisdom involves embracing this profound pursuit as a daily practice, applying ancient Gnostic teachings to cultivate inner clarity, discernment, and a life in harmony with the divine.

To walk the path of wisdom, the practitioner begins with a reflective understanding of detachment from the material world. In Gnosticism, the material realm is seen as a veil, a world that often distracts from the deeper, spiritual truths. Wisdom encourages the seeker to see beyond these distractions, recognizing them for what they are—temporary, fleeting, and ultimately incapable of bringing lasting fulfillment. Practitioners are encouraged to reflect on the transient nature of possessions, achievements, and even personal identity, grounding their purpose instead in the timeless essence of their soul. Through this detachment, the seeker develops a perspective that frees them from unnecessary desires and anxieties, aligning their focus with what is essential and enduring.

The practice of self-observation is also central to wisdom on the Gnostic path. Self-observation requires a heightened awareness of thoughts, actions, and emotions, allowing the practitioner to discern between impulses rooted in ego and those that spring from the soul's higher wisdom. This practice is not about self-judgment; rather, it is a compassionate witnessing of the self. As the practitioner becomes attuned to the flow of their inner world, they learn to recognize patterns—such as impatience, fear, or attachment—that cloud the spirit. With gentle awareness, these patterns are acknowledged and released, creating space for greater insight.

To cultivate this state, the seeker may engage in a simple daily meditation practice focused on reflective detachment. Sitting in silence, the practitioner watches thoughts arise and pass, observing them as one might watch clouds drift across the sky. Without grasping or rejecting any thought, the practitioner gently disengages from the mental chatter, becoming an observer of their own mind. This reflective detachment reveals to the seeker the nature of their inner dialogue, illuminating where they are easily swayed by desires or distractions, and allowing them to step into a place of peace and clarity.

The teachings of Gnostic wisdom also emphasize practical philosophy for daily life. Gnosticism is not a philosophy removed from life's realities but one that seeks to transform every moment into an opportunity for inner growth. Practitioners are encouraged to approach each day as a chance to apply their spiritual insights in simple, grounded ways. This could mean responding with patience rather than frustration in challenging situations, practicing kindness toward others, or making decisions with integrity, guided by an inner sense of rightness. By practicing these small acts of wisdom, the seeker begins to embody Gnostic principles in their interactions, cultivating a harmonious life that reflects the balance they are striving for within.

In addition to these practices, the seeker is introduced to the Gnostic concept of divine truth, which is seen not as a single dogmatic belief but as an ever-evolving awareness, a continual uncovering of the soul's deepest insights. Divine truth in Gnosticism is fluid, allowing the seeker to engage with multiple perspectives and remain open to new revelations. Through regular meditation and contemplation, the practitioner learns to listen to the subtle voice within that speaks of the highest truths. In this way, wisdom becomes a path of inquiry rather than certainty, a journey of ever-deepening understanding rather than rigid adherence to fixed ideas.

As the seeker engages with these teachings, they may begin a journaling practice focused on reflective insights and wisdom teachings. Journaling allows the practitioner to record moments of clarity and insight, creating a personal map of their spiritual journey. They might write about daily experiences that challenged or inspired them, recording how they applied wisdom in each situation and what they learned from it. This reflective exercise becomes a mirror for the soul, showing the practitioner how their understanding of wisdom is evolving and providing a sacred space to capture revelations that might otherwise pass unnoticed.

Symbolic meditation also becomes a valuable tool on the path of wisdom. This involves choosing a symbol that represents wisdom to the seeker—such as a flame, an owl, or an ancient tree—and meditating upon it with focus and reverence. The chosen symbol serves as a focal point, a doorway into the soul's wisdom. During meditation, the practitioner visualizes this symbol, allowing it to reveal layers of meaning, inspiring thoughts, images, or insights. Over time, the symbol becomes an anchor for wisdom, a familiar presence that reminds the practitioner of their commitment to a life of deeper understanding.

In moments of decision-making, the practitioner can turn to silent reflection, a practice that enables them to pause, breathe, and consult their inner wisdom before choosing a course of action. Instead of reacting impulsively, the seeker reflects on the motivations driving their choices, asking questions like "Does this align with my highest purpose?" or "Will this action bring harmony or create discord?" By cultivating this practice of inner consultation, the seeker learns to respond to life from a place of centered awareness, honoring the soul's wisdom rather than the fleeting impulses of the ego.

Over time, as these practices become integrated, the seeker may experience a shift in their perspective of the world. The material and superficial lose their grip, replaced by a deep appreciation for the essence of things. Relationships deepen, not because of dependency or need, but through an authentic connection that resonates from soul to soul. The seeker's inner life becomes one of peace and quiet insight, a state where the wisdom within speaks more loudly than the distractions without. They become a vessel for the light of gnosis, embodying a wisdom that draws them ever closer to the mysteries of the divine.

The path of wisdom is a journey without end, a continual turning inward to uncover what lies beneath, to touch the heart of truth and bring it forth in every thought, word, and deed. In these small, quiet practices, the Gnostic practitioner finds that wisdom is not something to be attained but a reflection of their deepest self, waiting always to be recognized and embodied.

Through each reflection, choice, and symbolic meditation, wisdom becomes not only a guiding light but a way of life, transforming the seeker and, in turn, the world around them. This journey is the essence of gnosis—the knowing that transcends knowledge, the illumination that burns brightly within, and the path that reveals the divine in every step.

In the deepening of the Gnostic path of wisdom, the seeker now moves from intellectual understanding to the integration of wisdom as a living principle within. This next step on the path involves cultivating practices that allow wisdom to become an inner compass, guiding actions, thoughts, and reflections in every moment. For the Gnostic, wisdom is not merely acquired; it is embodied, and through this embodiment, it transforms the practitioner's way of being.

The practice of contemplative reflection offers a profound tool for this integration, encouraging the seeker to create time each day to quietly reflect on the wisdom they have encountered and applied. In this practice, the practitioner sits in silence, reflecting on experiences from the day that required discernment, patience, or clarity. Each reflection is approached with gentle curiosity, observing how choices aligned—or did not—with the wisdom that guides the soul. Through regular practice, contemplative reflection becomes a ritual of self-inquiry, helping the seeker refine their understanding and internalize the lessons each experience offers.

To deepen this journey, the practitioner may employ wisdom-based meditation exercises. These meditations focus on anchoring Gnostic principles, such as humility, compassion, and openness to divine guidance. For example, a meditation on humility might involve visualizing oneself surrounded by light, feeling the warmth of the divine illuminating the soul. In this light, the practitioner allows any feelings of self-importance or fear to dissolve, inviting in the quality of humility—a state of deep openness that allows wisdom to flow freely. With each meditation, the practitioner internalizes these principles, carrying them into daily life as a living embodiment of the path.

Another powerful tool in deepening wisdom is the practice of inner listening, an exercise that connects the seeker with the voice of the Higher Self, the divine essence within that holds eternal knowledge. Inner listening begins with quieting the mind through focused breathing, then turning attention inward, as if listening to a faint, wise voice that speaks from the depths of the heart. In this silence, the practitioner may ask questions or reflect on decisions, allowing insights to emerge naturally. By trusting this inner voice, the seeker strengthens the connection to their own wellspring of wisdom, an intuitive compass that guides them toward choices aligned with their highest good.

For Gnostic practitioners, integrating wisdom also involves living with intentional simplicity, an approach that emphasizes the value of clarity and purpose in both thought and action. This is not simply an exercise in minimalism but a conscious choice to prioritize what truly serves the soul's journey. The practitioner might start by examining how they spend their time, asking, "Is this activity or relationship nourishing my soul?" Through this self-inquiry, they gradually simplify their lives, making space for experiences that deepen understanding and connection rather than distractions that draw them from their path.

As the seeker embraces simplicity, they also adopt the practice of observing inner silence, a state of peacefulness where the mind is stilled, and the inner world becomes quiet. This silence is not empty but filled with the potential for insight, a clear space where the soul's wisdom can be heard without interference. The seeker may enter this silence during meditation or moments of solitude, simply observing the mind without judgment, letting thoughts drift like clouds. Through the discipline of silence, the practitioner creates an inner sanctuary, a place where wisdom flourishes and guides each step of the journey.

To make wisdom a fully integrated aspect of their being, the practitioner can engage in acts of mindful service. Service in this context is not limited to helping others but also includes acts of kindness, compassion, and integrity in everyday interactions. By approaching each encounter with mindfulness, the seeker honors the divine within themselves and others, creating a space where wisdom flows naturally. Whether offering guidance to a friend, extending patience to a stranger, or showing gratitude, each act of mindful service reinforces wisdom as a living practice, a way to honor the interconnectedness of all beings.

A practice that brings profound insights into the Gnostic seeker's life is journaling for wisdom integration, an exercise that helps solidify understanding and recognize patterns over time. After moments of reflection or after a challenging experience, the seeker writes down what they observed, the decisions made, and how these choices aligned with their highest principles. This journal becomes a sacred record, allowing the practitioner to witness their growth in wisdom, learning from moments of clarity as well as from mistakes. By revisiting these entries, the seeker gains perspective on their journey, seeing how each challenge has contributed to their unfolding understanding.

The Gnostic practitioner also learns to deepen wisdom by practicing acceptance and surrender, recognizing that true wisdom often lies in letting go of control and allowing the divine to work through life's circumstances. Surrender does not mean passivity; rather, it is an active choice to trust that each moment contains what is needed for the soul's growth. In moments of uncertainty or difficulty, the seeker practices acceptance, viewing each experience as a teacher. This surrender opens the practitioner to unexpected insights, as they become a vessel for the divine wisdom that transcends the limitations of the personal self.

Finally, the path of wisdom includes contemplating the mysteries of divine truth, engaging with the infinite questions that inspire humility and wonder. The seeker may spend time contemplating concepts like the nature of the soul, the meaning of life, or the purpose of suffering. These reflections are not meant to yield concrete answers but to open the practitioner to an ever-deepening awareness of the divine mysteries. By embracing questions without the need for definitive answers, the seeker cultivates an openness that allows wisdom to reveal itself in countless ways, deepening their understanding with each experience.

In this advanced stage of the path of wisdom, the practitioner no longer sees wisdom as a distant goal but as an essential, integrated part of their life and consciousness. Each practice—whether meditation, contemplation, service, or simplicity—becomes a thread in the fabric of the soul, weaving together a life that reflects the divine light within. Through daily acts, silent reflection, and inner surrender, the practitioner embodies wisdom, becoming a beacon of clarity, insight, and compassion for others.

In this way, the Gnostic seeker transforms, finding that the journey toward wisdom is not one of acquiring something new but of revealing what has always been present within. Wisdom becomes not merely a guiding principle but the essence of the seeker's being, illuminating each step of the Gnostic path and drawing them ever closer to the ultimate truth.

As the seeker progresses, wisdom becomes a constant presence, informing decisions, deepening relationships, and inspiring actions that resonate with the divine. Through the living practice of wisdom, the Gnostic practitioner experiences a profound harmony with the world, sensing the sacred in all things and embracing each moment as an expression of divine truth.

Chapter 11
Mysteries of the Demiurge

In the teachings of Gnosticism, the Demiurge occupies a central role as a complex and enigmatic figure, often portrayed as an imperfect creator presiding over the material world. For the Gnostic seeker, understanding the nature of the Demiurge is essential, as it illuminates the obstacles that obscure the soul's journey toward the divine. Through this exploration, the practitioner learns to recognize the illusions woven by the Demiurge and discovers the means to transcend them, moving closer to the light of gnosis.

The concept of the Demiurge originates in ancient Gnostic texts, where he is depicted as a lesser divinity, sometimes known as Yaldabaoth or Saklas, who believes himself to be the sole creator. Unlike the divine fullness, or Pleroma, from which the soul originates, the Demiurge is associated with the material realm—a world characterized by duality, separation, and illusion. He is often imagined as the architect of the physical universe, but his creations, although beautiful and intricate, are flawed reflections of the true divine light. This misalignment results in a world that, while captivating, distracts the soul from its higher purpose.

To begin uncovering the mysteries of the Demiurge, the practitioner first reflects on the material world as a realm of duality and illusion. The Demiurge's creation is, at its core, an illusion—an intricate tapestry woven with both light and shadow, where the soul's divine origin is often forgotten or obscured. The Gnostic practitioner learns to observe the world without being entangled in its drama, seeing beyond appearances to perceive the soul's true essence beneath the surface of worldly desires, fears, and attachments. By acknowledging that the material realm is a veil, the seeker cultivates a state of inner detachment, recognizing that true fulfillment cannot be found in the impermanent, external world.

The Demiurge's influence is not limited to the material world alone; it extends into the human psyche, manifesting as ego, pride, and the belief in separation. This part of the journey requires the practitioner to practice inner discernment, recognizing thoughts, habits, and desires that stem from the ego—the inner Demiurge—rather than the soul. This discernment involves examining one's motives, questioning whether they are inspired by the search for truth and compassion, or by the ego's need for control, validation, or superiority. By observing these aspects of the self with honesty and compassion, the practitioner becomes adept at identifying the Demiurge's subtle influence within, gradually loosening its hold over their inner world.

In exploring the Demiurge, Gnostic texts often speak of the concept of the "false self", an identity constructed from societal expectations, fears, and material pursuits. This false self, or persona, is a mask that obscures the soul's divine spark. Through contemplative practices, the practitioner seeks to see beyond this mask, understanding that their true essence is not defined by labels, achievements, or material possessions. By peeling back these layers, the seeker uncovers a deeper self, a soul that exists beyond the illusions imposed by the material realm and the Demiurge's influence.

At this stage, the Gnostic practitioner is encouraged to engage in meditative practices to separate the self from illusion. One such practice involves visualizing the self as surrounded by a dense mist, symbolic of the illusions and influences of the Demiurge. As the practitioner breathes deeply and centers their awareness, they imagine this mist dissipating, revealing a radiant, inner light—their true essence. This light is untouched by the external world, a reflection of the Pleroma's divine fullness.

Through regular practice, the seeker strengthens this inner connection, gaining clarity and cultivating resilience against the seductive power of the Demiurge's illusions.

As the seeker grows in understanding, they also reflect on the concept of suffering and limitation, which are often attributed to the Demiurge's imperfect creation. In the Gnostic view, suffering and struggle are not mere punishments or tests but invitations to transcend. When the practitioner encounters limitations, whether physical, emotional, or circumstantial, they are encouraged to look beyond the surface, seeing each challenge as a lesson in detachment, compassion, or resilience. This reframing of suffering transforms it from an oppressive weight into a catalyst for inner growth, helping the soul to release attachments and align more fully with its divine purpose.

Understanding the Demiurge also involves exploring the notion of freedom within a bound world. Although the Demiurge is seen as a force that restricts, Gnostic teachings emphasize that true freedom lies not in escaping the material world, but in transcending its influence. The seeker learns that freedom is an internal state, achieved not by abandoning responsibilities or relationships, but by engaging with them from a place of awareness and detachment. In this way, the practitioner becomes a free soul within a bound world, navigating life with clarity and compassion without succumbing to its illusions.

To deepen this exploration, the practitioner may work with symbolic rituals that represent the soul's journey from the darkness of ignorance to the light of gnosis. One such ritual might involve lighting a single candle in a dark room, symbolizing the soul's inner light that shines even within the shadowed realm of the Demiurge. The practitioner sits in silence, focusing on the flame and allowing it to represent the divine essence within, a spark that cannot be extinguished by any external force. This simple ritual affirms the presence of the true self, a self that remains connected to the Pleroma even as it navigates the material world.

Finally, the mysteries of the Demiurge teach the seeker to embrace compassionate awareness. By understanding that the Demiurge, like humanity, is an imperfect reflection of the divine, the practitioner is reminded of the importance of compassion. The flaws and limitations observed in the world are not to be condemned but to be understood as part of the soul's journey to wholeness. This compassion extends to oneself and others, cultivating an understanding that, while the material realm may be imperfect, it serves as a mirror for the soul's growth and awakening.

Through this compassionate awareness, the practitioner transforms their perception of the Demiurge. No longer seen merely as an adversary or a source of suffering, the Demiurge is understood as a symbol of the soul's journey through limitation and illusion. In transcending the Demiurge's influence, the seeker does not reject the world but sees it clearly, embracing each experience as an opportunity to deepen wisdom and strengthen their connection with the divine.

In these reflections and practices, the mysteries of the Demiurge invite the Gnostic seeker to look beyond the surface of reality, to question, discern, and ultimately, to transcend. Through meditation, discernment, and compassion, the practitioner learns to navigate the material world with clarity and purpose, each step moving them closer to the Pleroma, the divine fullness from which they originated.

This exploration is not a rejection of the world but a transformation of perception, a way of seeing beyond illusion to glimpse the divine essence within all things. As the seeker moves through these mysteries, they come to understand that the light of gnosis shines even in the darkest corners of creation, guiding the soul back to its source, beyond the Demiurge's reach, and into the infinite unity of the divine.

In further exploration of the Demiurge's mysteries, the Gnostic seeker delves into the intricate relationships between the Demiurge, the Pleroma, and the intermediary entities that bridge the material and spiritual realms. Understanding these dynamics offers a path to overcoming the illusions and challenges of the material world, a journey through which the practitioner strengthens their alignment with divine wisdom. This chapter expands upon the Demiurge's role, focusing on how the seeker can navigate the subtle spiritual challenges posed by his influence and deepen their connection to the Pleroma—the boundless, divine fullness.

Central to this understanding is the relationship between the Demiurge and the Pleroma. While the Demiurge presides over the physical realm, the Pleroma represents divine completeness, a state of ultimate unity and harmony that transcends the material limitations imposed by the Demiurge's creations. The seeker comes to understand that the Demiurge, despite his role as a creator, is disconnected from this divine fullness. This lack of awareness results in a realm bound by duality, where limitations and oppositions distract the soul from its true nature. Recognizing this separation helps the practitioner to distinguish between the world of appearances and the divine essence that exists beyond it.

To deepen this insight, the Gnostic seeker is guided to reflect on the concept of spiritual ignorance, often symbolized by the Demiurge's limited perception. Unlike the Pleroma, which is defined by omniscience and unity, the Demiurge operates within a narrow awareness, convinced of his own completeness yet blind to the divine fullness that lies beyond his reach. In recognizing this spiritual ignorance, the practitioner is reminded of the ways in which human consciousness, too, is often clouded by ego and attachment. Through practices of self-reflection and humility, the seeker learns to identify these limitations within, consciously working to dissolve them and expand their awareness toward the wisdom of the Pleroma.

One effective approach for transcending the influence of the Demiurge is the practice of invoking the Aeons, intermediary entities that represent divine aspects within the Pleroma. Each Aeon embodies a specific quality, such as truth, love, wisdom, or courage, offering the seeker a bridge between the material world and the spiritual reality of the Pleroma. By contemplating or meditating on these divine aspects, the practitioner begins to align their inner self with the qualities of the Pleroma, inviting these energies to dispel the Demiurge's influence within their psyche. Through this connection with the Aeons, the seeker strengthens their inner light, fostering virtues that transcend the illusions of the material realm.

In this expanded understanding, the Gnostic practitioner engages in rituals that invoke the qualities of the Aeons. For instance, a ritual focused on wisdom may involve lighting a candle and calling upon the Aeon of Sophia, embodying divine wisdom. As the flame burns, the practitioner meditates upon the quality of wisdom, visualizing it illuminating their inner self and dissolving the shadows cast by the ego and material desires. This invocation acts as a purification ritual, clearing the mind of distractions and aligning the heart with the essence of divine wisdom. Through regular practice, the seeker becomes increasingly receptive to these qualities, integrating them into their life and actions.

Another advanced practice involves exploring the illusions of the material world through the lens of the Demiurge's creation. In Gnostic understanding, the physical realm often presents illusions that appear meaningful or fulfilling but ultimately keep the soul bound to transient desires. By identifying these illusions—such as the pursuit of wealth, power, or fame—the practitioner trains themselves to see beyond them, recognizing that true fulfillment lies not in accumulation or status, but in inner liberation and divine connection. This exercise in discernment transforms the way the seeker interacts with the world, approaching it as a school for spiritual growth rather than as a source of permanent satisfaction.

To further navigate the Demiurge's illusions, the practitioner may engage in contemplative exercises designed to reveal the transient nature of material experiences. One practice involves visualizing the self as a traveler moving through a marketplace filled with distractions and temptations. The seeker imagines passing by each one without attachment, moving forward with clear purpose, aware that their true destination lies beyond these temptations. This visualization strengthens the will, training the practitioner to resist the pull of external illusions and remain focused on their inner journey.

The mysteries of the Demiurge also teach the practitioner about the importance of inner alignment with the divine spark, the soul's connection to the Pleroma. Despite the limitations imposed by the material world, each soul carries within it a spark of divine light, a fragment of the Pleroma that cannot be extinguished or corrupted. Through meditation, the practitioner visualizes this inner light growing stronger, expanding within until it fills the entire being, dispelling the shadows of ignorance and fear. This light becomes a beacon, guiding the soul beyond the Demiurge's reach and affirming the practitioner's true nature as a being of divine origin.

In strengthening their connection to this inner light, the seeker cultivates an understanding of spiritual sovereignty, the recognition that their soul's essence remains untouched by the Demiurge's influence. This sovereignty is a form of liberation, empowering the practitioner to navigate the world with a sense of inner freedom and resilience. The seeker understands that while they must engage with the physical realm, they are not bound by its limitations. This shift in perspective allows the practitioner to view challenges as opportunities for growth, a perspective rooted in the eternal rather than the ephemeral.

In moments of doubt or spiritual fatigue, the Gnostic seeker may turn to contemplative communion with the Pleroma, visualizing themselves surrounded by the fullness of divine light, embraced by the Aeons who embody its virtues. This practice fosters a deep sense of reassurance, a reminder that the soul's origin and destination are within the divine reality of the Pleroma, untouched by the imperfections of the material world. Through this communion, the practitioner experiences the comfort and clarity of gnosis, an understanding that they are never alone on their journey, for the Pleroma is both within and around them, guiding and supporting their every step.

This advanced exploration of the Demiurge also involves a reflection on the purpose of material limitations. In Gnostic thought, the limitations imposed by the Demiurge, while challenging, serve as catalysts for the soul's awakening. Each obstacle, distraction, or attachment presents the soul with an opportunity to choose discernment, compassion, and understanding over illusion. In this way, the Demiurge, despite his ignorance, inadvertently serves the soul's growth, as each challenge inspires the practitioner to remember and strengthen their connection with the divine.

Through these reflections and practices, the seeker comes to see the Demiurge not as an enemy but as a symbol of the necessary struggles and illusions that each soul must overcome. This realization frees the practitioner from a dualistic perspective, allowing them to transcend the polarities of light and dark, viewing all experiences as part of the journey toward unity with the divine.

As the seeker moves beyond the Demiurge's realm, they find that each insight and virtue gained along the way contributes to a greater wholeness. Through inner light, communion with the Pleroma, and the strength of spiritual sovereignty, the practitioner ascends beyond illusion, embracing the divine fullness of their true essence. The mysteries of the Demiurge reveal themselves as mirrors, reflecting the seeker's own capacity for transformation, and guiding them toward the realization of their eternal unity with the Pleroma.

Chapter 12
Purification Rituals

The practice of purification is a cornerstone of Gnostic spirituality, preparing the practitioner's body, mind, and spirit to become a clear vessel for divine wisdom. Purification is more than a cleansing ritual; it is a conscious act of aligning oneself with the higher realms, clearing away the denser energies of the material world to allow for a profound communion with the soul's essence. This chapter introduces the Gnostic seeker to foundational purification practices that release accumulated energies, providing clarity, lightness, and focus as they advance on their spiritual journey.

Purification begins with the cleansing of the physical body, a practice that recognizes the body as a sacred instrument for spiritual experience. The practitioner is encouraged to take an intentional, meditative approach to personal care, beginning with practices such as mindful bathing or washing hands and face with the intention of clearing away the physical and energetic impurities encountered throughout the day. In this process, water is revered not merely as a substance but as a symbol of purification and renewal, a conduit for the sacred. While washing, the seeker visualizes any dense energies dissolving, washed away by the water, leaving a sense of lightness and rejuvenation.

A further purification practice involves the use of herbal baths to enhance the cleansing process. Traditionally, certain herbs, such as sage, rosemary, or lavender, are steeped in warm water to create a fragrant bath that purifies both body and spirit. As the practitioner immerses themselves in the bath, they meditate on the properties of each herb, acknowledging its purpose—sage for clearing, rosemary for focus, lavender for calm. This ritual creates a sensory experience that harmonizes body, mind, and spirit, cultivating a state of receptivity and serenity. Each herb brings its own unique essence, serving as an ally in the seeker's purification and preparation for deeper spiritual work.

In addition to physical cleansing, breathwork plays a vital role in Gnostic purification practices. Breath is viewed as the life force that connects the physical to the spiritual, a rhythm that aligns the body with the divine essence. The practitioner begins by sitting quietly, inhaling deeply and exhaling slowly, releasing any tension or stagnant energy with each breath. This simple, rhythmic breathing gradually brings the seeker's awareness into the present moment, dissolving distractions and opening inner space for clarity and insight. Inhale by inhale, exhale by exhale, the seeker connects with the life force, feeling more centered and purified with each cycle.

Another powerful tool for purification is smudging with sacred herbs or incense. Smudging involves burning a bundle of sage, cedar, palo santo, or frankincense, allowing the smoke to drift through the air, surrounding the practitioner and purifying the space. The seeker may hold the smudge stick and gently wave it around themselves, focusing on areas where they feel dense or stagnant energy, such as around the heart or the third eye. As the smoke rises, they visualize it carrying away any energetic impurities, allowing them to feel cleansed and protected. This ritual can also be performed in a room or entire home, ensuring the space is free from residual energies that may interfere with meditation or other spiritual practices.

An extension of smudging is the use of crystals and stones for purification. Crystals such as clear quartz, selenite, and black tourmaline are commonly used for their purifying properties. The practitioner holds the crystal in their hand or places it on their altar, setting the intention for it to absorb any dense or stagnant energies. Some practitioners may also carry a small purifying crystal with them throughout the day as a protective amulet, feeling its grounding presence as a subtle shield against external influences. Regularly cleansing and charging these crystals, perhaps by placing them under sunlight or moonlight, ensures that they continue to serve their purifying role effectively.

The Gnostic seeker is also encouraged to cultivate a purified mental state through mindfulness and meditative focus. Throughout daily life, thoughts and emotions often accumulate, clouding the mind and preventing it from accessing deeper spiritual insight. To clear this mental clutter, the practitioner can perform a simple purification visualization, imagining a gentle rain washing through the mind, carrying away worries, judgments, and preoccupations. As this inner rain flows, the practitioner feels their mind becoming calm, clear, and receptive, a state conducive to insight and communion with the divine. This mental purification becomes a daily habit, a practice that helps the seeker maintain clarity and balance.

Another technique for mental purification involves chanting a mantra or sacred word. Repeating a simple, sacred sound like "OM" or "HU" calms the mind, aligning the seeker's energy with divine vibrations. As the mantra is softly spoken or chanted, it resonates within the body, dissolving mental distractions and establishing a state of focused presence. Through repetition, the practitioner feels their thoughts quieting, replaced by a sense of peace and connection. The chosen mantra acts as a spiritual tool, clearing away thought forms that cloud perception and grounding the seeker in a state of inner stillness.

In the practice of spatial purification, the practitioner extends the purifying process to their surroundings. This might involve decluttering a personal space, ensuring that the environment reflects clarity and harmony. The seeker may arrange their space with intentionality, placing objects that inspire peace and spiritual focus, such as candles, crystals, or sacred images. A simple ritual of lighting a candle and focusing on its flame for a few moments at the beginning of the day can reinforce this sacred atmosphere, creating a clear space where the divine is welcomed and honored.

The Gnostic path encourages emotional purification, a process that involves acknowledging and releasing emotions that no longer serve the soul's growth. In moments of solitude, the practitioner reflects on any lingering feelings—resentments, fears, or attachments—that weigh on the heart. Through journaling, meditation, or quiet reflection, they give these emotions space to be acknowledged without judgment, allowing them to surface and dissolve. This compassionate self-observation creates emotional spaciousness, helping the practitioner to forgive and release, creating a clear inner space for the soul's light to shine unobstructed.

As the practitioner incorporates these purification rituals into their daily life, they begin to feel a shift within—a lightness, a clarity, a deeper connection to their true essence. Purification becomes not a single act but an ongoing process, a daily alignment with the divine. Each ritual, each breath, each moment of mindful cleansing brings the seeker closer to their soul's true nature, allowing them to approach life from a place of calm and focused awareness.

Through these practices, the seeker cultivates an inner and outer world that supports their spiritual growth, a world in which they feel both protected and aligned with the higher truths of Gnosticism. As they continue on this path, purification becomes second nature, a part of their daily rhythm that prepares them for deeper explorations, higher states of consciousness, and a life rooted in clarity, insight, and divine alignment. Each layer of cleansing unveils more of the soul's divine light, bringing the practitioner closer to the mysteries that lie beyond the veil of the material.

With the foundation of daily purification practices established, the Gnostic seeker now delves into more advanced methods for creating a clear, receptive vessel for spiritual illumination. These deeper rituals involve symbolic and spiritual elements that resonate with the soul's higher vibrations, fortifying the practitioner's energy field and aligning their entire being with the divine. In this advanced purification work, the seeker moves beyond personal cleansing to engage with protective entities, powerful symbols, and focused rituals that elevate and intensify the connection with the divine.

At this stage, purification involves an intricate ritual of consecrating sacred symbols and items, imbuing them with spiritual power that fortifies the seeker's environment. The practitioner begins by selecting objects that resonate with protection and purity—such as a crystal, a small statue, or a symbol of light—and dedicating these items through an act of consecration. This ritual might include lighting incense, sprinkling purified water, and holding each item while repeating a simple invocation, such as, "May this item be blessed with divine light and protect this space." Through this consecration, each object becomes more than a mere symbol; it holds the essence of the divine, serving as a constant source of protection and energy renewal.

One significant practice in advanced purification is the invocation of protective entities. In Gnostic tradition, certain spiritual beings are considered protectors who can aid the seeker in dispelling negative energies. Angels, archangels, and certain divine archetypes embody qualities of strength, wisdom, and purity. The practitioner may call upon these entities through a focused ritual, standing in a sacred space and invoking their presence with reverence. For instance, they might call upon the Archangel Michael, visualizing a powerful, radiant light surrounding them, forming a protective shield. This light is both a defense and a cleanser, dissolving any lingering energies that do not serve the soul's highest purpose. Such invocations allow the practitioner to feel supported by the divine, grounding them in a sense of spiritual safety.

Further refining their space, the seeker may create a personal altar for purification, a dedicated space that embodies purity, calm, and protection. This altar might include candles, sacred images, purifying stones, and symbols that hold personal meaning. Each time the practitioner approaches the altar, they are reminded of their commitment to spiritual clarity and higher consciousness. Lighting a candle at this altar each morning or evening becomes a daily ritual, a gesture of devotion and purification that sets the tone for the day or night. In this way, the altar becomes an anchor, a place where the practitioner can return to center, grounded in the energy of their spiritual intention.

Advanced purification also incorporates the use of sacred symbols in visualization practices. One powerful symbol in Gnostic purification is the circle of light, representing unity, protection, and divine presence. To create this symbol in their purification practice, the practitioner envisions a brilliant circle of light surrounding them, spinning gently as it repels any disruptive energies. This visualization can be reinforced by drawing a small circle on a piece of paper or tracing it in the air, a gesture that further solidifies the protective field around them. Over time, this symbolic circle becomes a living shield, called upon whenever the seeker feels the need for protection or grounding.

Another potent tool for advanced purification is chanting specific protection mantras or sacred words from the Gnostic tradition. Words like "Sophia," symbolizing wisdom, or "Pleroma," the fullness of divine light, are intoned with reverence, resonating within the practitioner's energy field and creating a powerful, cleansing vibration. Chanting serves as both a shield and a harmonizer, aligning the practitioner's inner self with divine energy and blocking the entry of any disruptive forces. The sound of the chant is allowed to vibrate through the body and mind, creating a state of calm, clarity, and resilience against external influences.

An important aspect of purification at this level is energetic cord-cutting, a ritual that releases attachments to energies, situations, or relationships that no longer serve the practitioner's spiritual growth. This practice is performed with great intention, often beginning with a quiet meditation in which the seeker visualizes any cords that may connect them to unresolved emotions, past experiences, or people who drain their energy. Once these connections are identified, the practitioner envisions a golden or silver blade of light severing each cord gently, releasing the energy back to its source. This ritual allows the practitioner to feel lighter, free from energetic attachments that could interfere with their inner peace and clarity.

In the exploration of advanced purification, the seeker may also work with elemental invocations to invoke the natural forces that cleanse and protect. This ritual involves calling upon the elements of earth, water, fire, and air, each representing a unique form of purification. Earth is visualized as grounding, drawing out dense energies; water is imagined as washing through the energy field, clearing emotional residue; fire burns away impurities; and air carries clarity and lightness. The practitioner may invoke each element in turn, sensing its qualities, and allowing its energy to work within them. By connecting to these elemental forces, the seeker aligns with the natural rhythms of the universe, reinforcing their own resilience and adaptability.

To integrate these advanced purification rituals, the Gnostic practitioner develops a daily practice of protective affirmations, which reinforce the intention of inner clarity and strength. Simple affirmations such as "I am a vessel of divine light" or "I release all energies that do not serve my highest purpose" are repeated with focus and conviction. These affirmations are not simply words but declarations of spiritual intent, reminders of the practitioner's commitment to remain aligned with their divine essence.

Another profound tool is purifying visualization journeys, where the practitioner mentally enters a sacred space—a serene forest, a mountain peak, or a pristine waterfall—where they envision themselves cleansed by the natural elements. In this inner landscape, they may walk barefoot on the earth, feel the gentle warmth of the sun, or immerse in a crystal-clear pool, allowing nature's purity to dissolve any tension or impurities within. These visualization journeys are powerful reminders of the soul's inherent purity, offering a momentary reprieve from the demands of the material world, where the seeker reconnects with their core essence.

With each practice, the seeker's energy becomes increasingly refined, resonating at a higher frequency that aligns with the divine. These purification rituals elevate the practitioner's awareness, clearing away the noise and disturbances of the outer world, allowing a closer communion with their higher self. Advanced purification becomes not only a preparation for spiritual work but a lifestyle, a continuous, conscious act of staying clear, focused, and deeply connected to the divine.

By cultivating these practices, the Gnostic practitioner transforms purification into a sacred art, an intentional way of life that prepares the soul for the mysteries ahead. Each ritual, whether performed daily or in moments of need, becomes a sanctuary for the soul—a space where the light of the divine flows freely, guiding the seeker toward greater understanding, harmony, and inner freedom. Through the journey of purification, the Gnostic path reveals itself as one of ever-deepening clarity and transcendence, a path that leads the seeker back to the fullness of the Pleroma and to the radiant essence within.

Chapter 13
Inner Light Meditation

The journey of Gnosticism leads each seeker toward the discovery and illumination of their own inner light, a spark of divine essence hidden beneath the layers of worldly experience and personal identity. Inner Light Meditation is a foundational practice in Gnosticism, inviting the practitioner to awaken and connect with this inner spark, guiding them closer to gnosis. In this chapter, the seeker learns techniques for recognizing and nurturing this inner light, preparing for deeper, transformative experiences that will unfold on their spiritual path.

The practice begins with a simple, but profoundly grounding, ritual of centering and breath awareness, allowing the practitioner to bring their focus inward and quiet the mind. Sitting in a relaxed yet upright position, the seeker closes their eyes, taking a few deep breaths to calm their body and ease any lingering tension. With each exhale, they release external distractions, and with each inhale, they draw their awareness inward. This focus on breath acts as a doorway, shifting attention from the outer world to the inner sanctuary, preparing the practitioner to connect with the radiant light within.

As the breath settles, the practitioner shifts into visualizing the inner light, the first step in consciously engaging with their divine essence. They might begin by imagining a small point of light at the center of the chest, often called the heart center, a symbol of the soul's connection to the divine. This light is visualized as soft, warm, and gentle, yet unwavering, like a candle flame that holds an eternal glow. With each breath, the practitioner envisions this light growing slightly brighter, expanding gently outward in all directions, radiating a sense of peace, safety, and spiritual clarity.

Throughout this meditation, the seeker focuses on strengthening the connection with this light, feeling it as a living presence within. The inner light may initially feel subtle, even elusive, but with steady attention, it grows more vivid, filling the entire chest with warmth and gentle brilliance. As this light expands, the practitioner experiences a sense of unity and wholeness, a reminder that this essence is their truest self—untouched by external influences, timeless, and pure. Over time, the inner light becomes a guide, a source of strength that can be called upon whenever the seeker needs clarity, peace, or inspiration.

The next phase involves deepening awareness of the light's qualities, noticing how it feels, not only within the heart but also as it begins to fill the entire body. As the light spreads, the practitioner may feel an uplifting warmth, a gentle vibration, or a feeling of profound calm. This sensation becomes an experience of communion with the divine, a moment where the seeker feels intimately connected to their own spiritual essence. In these moments, the inner light is not just a visualization but a felt experience, a state of being that transcends the mind's limitations.

In Gnostic practice, it's common to use a mantra or sacred word to enhance this inner light meditation. One might choose a word such as "Sophia" (representing divine wisdom) or "Lux" (Latin for light) to help focus and elevate the mind. Softly repeating this word, either out loud or mentally, the practitioner allows it to resonate within the body, feeling it harmonize with the light within. Each repetition strengthens the connection, aligning the seeker's entire being with this essence of light and wisdom. The mantra becomes a rhythmic expression of the divine, deepening the sense of peace and unity.

As the inner light continues to expand, the practitioner visualizes it radiating beyond the body, creating a protective aura that surrounds and shields them. This aura of light forms a boundary of peace and purity, keeping them centered and safe. Through this practice, the seeker develops a protective field that can be drawn upon whenever they feel exposed to disruptive energies or are in need of grounding. This aura is not merely a shield; it is a radiant expression of their inner essence, a reminder of their connection to the divine even in challenging moments.

In time, this meditation evolves into a practice of sustained awareness of the light, where the practitioner learns to carry this sense of inner illumination beyond the meditation session and into their daily life. They begin to approach each experience with an awareness of this light within, seeing through its clear perspective, whether in moments of peace or conflict. This ongoing awareness allows the practitioner to view themselves and others from a place of compassion and understanding, recognizing the divine spark in all.

For those new to Inner Light Meditation, it can be helpful to incorporate a guided visualization, imagining oneself in a sacred setting, such as a quiet temple, an ancient forest, or a mountain peak bathed in light. Within this setting, the seeker envisions a divine being or sacred symbol radiating light, which they then absorb, allowing it to fill their entire being. This practice helps the mind relax into a receptive state, allowing the practitioner to connect with their inner light in a vivid, inspiring way. Over time, the need for this visualization fades, as the seeker becomes accustomed to connecting with their light directly.

The transformative nature of Inner Light Meditation extends beyond the meditation itself, shaping how the practitioner views their purpose and experiences in life. With consistent practice, the inner light becomes a steady presence that offers insight, strength, and resilience. The seeker begins to understand that this light is a part of the divine Pleroma, a spark of the boundless fullness that exists beyond the material world. This realization deepens their commitment to the Gnostic path, inspiring them to live in alignment with this light, embodying its qualities in all aspects of life.

As the practitioner progresses, the light within becomes an inner teacher, illuminating the mind and heart, revealing truths that might otherwise remain hidden. This light offers guidance in moments of uncertainty, bringing clarity when emotions or thoughts cloud the way. In this way, the inner light becomes an invaluable companion, a source of wisdom that leads the practitioner ever closer to the mysteries of gnosis.

Each meditation is a step deeper into the self, a journey into the divine essence within, and a reminder of the ultimate unity of all existence. Through Inner Light Meditation, the Gnostic seeker learns not only to recognize this light but to dwell within it, living each moment as an expression of the divine radiance that they have discovered within themselves.

Building on the foundational practice of connecting with the inner light, the seeker now learns to expand and utilize this illumination across the entire spiritual body. This phase of Inner Light Meditation guides the practitioner in spreading this divine spark through different energy centers and, ultimately, using this light as a source of healing, protection, and profound spiritual insight. By nurturing and guiding this inner light, the practitioner transforms it into a wellspring of spiritual power, enabling deeper experiences of gnosis and expanded states of consciousness.

At this stage, the meditation begins as before, with breath awareness and centering, focusing inward and visualizing a point of light at the heart center. Once the mind is calm and focused, the practitioner visualizes this light expanding beyond the heart, moving gently up and down through the body's energy centers. Starting at the base of the spine and moving upward, each center or "chakra" is visualized as a vibrant sphere of light, with the inner light activating, energizing, and aligning these centers. As each center becomes illuminated, the practitioner feels a gentle warmth and vibrancy, as if each part of the body and spirit is waking up to its own inner wisdom.

This expansion through the energy centers cultivates a full-bodied awareness of the divine light within, creating a sense of wholeness and alignment. The practitioner feels the light permeating the root, sacral, solar plexus, heart, throat, third eye, and crown centers, uniting the physical and spiritual aspects of their being. This process not only harmonizes the energy centers but also fosters a profound sense of balance, aligning the seeker's physical, mental, and spiritual selves. As the light reaches the crown, it connects with the higher realms, symbolizing the soul's continuous link to the divine Pleroma.

Following this activation, the practitioner shifts to spreading the inner light throughout the body's entire energy field. Visualizing the light radiating from each energy center, they imagine it extending outward, filling every cell and every space within. This light moves freely, washing through the body like a gentle wave, cleansing, healing, and energizing each area it touches. This process is often experienced as a deep inner peace, a sensation of warmth and lightness as denser energies dissipate and the body is infused with renewed life force. Each breath strengthens this radiant field, creating a profound sense of unity and invigoration.

An important aspect of this stage is using the inner light for protection and grounding. The practitioner visualizes their entire body surrounded by a luminous shield, a cocoon of light that keeps their energy pure and centered. This protective layer serves as a barrier against disruptive or unwanted energies, reinforcing their spiritual sovereignty. As the practitioner moves through their daily life, this shield can be invoked at any time by reconnecting with the inner light, feeling its warmth and strength as a reminder of the divine presence that resides within.

As this practice becomes integrated, the practitioner learns to extend the inner light outward for healing, both for themselves and others. To do this, they begin by focusing on an area of the body or an aspect of the self that requires healing or clarity. They visualize the light moving intentionally to this area, concentrating its warmth and purity, allowing it to dissolve blockages, pain, or negative thought patterns. This healing light is not directed by force but is allowed to flow naturally, guided by the intention for wholeness and balance. In this way, the practitioner experiences their inner light as an active force of restoration, a source of comfort and support on their path.

Beyond self-healing, the Gnostic seeker learns to extend this light toward others, using the power of intention and compassion. When visualizing another person, the practitioner imagines them surrounded by the same radiant light, offering warmth, healing, and clarity. This practice is done from a place of non-attachment, with respect for the other's journey, and with the simple intention to share peace and wellness. The light flows naturally, connecting with the other person's energy field without imposing. This practice of shared light reminds the practitioner of the interconnectedness of all souls, allowing them to serve as a vessel of divine presence.

An advanced technique at this level is using the inner light to access higher states of consciousness and wisdom. Once the light has filled the body and energy centers, the practitioner focuses on the crown center, visualizing the light reaching upward, extending beyond the physical realm. Through this connection, the seeker feels their consciousness expanding, as if their inner light were merging with the infinite light of the Pleroma. In this space of pure connection, insights and intuitions may arise—flashes of understanding, images, or even words that speak directly to the heart. Here, the seeker experiences an unfiltered glimpse of divine wisdom, a state of gnosis that transcends intellectual knowledge.

During these moments, the practitioner allows themselves to rest in the state of illumination, feeling the fullness of being that comes with direct experience of the divine. This state is not forced but entered through surrender, allowing the light to guide the experience. It is in these quiet, illuminated moments that the practitioner may sense their deepest connection to the divine, a communion that feels timeless and infinite. This state of being remains imprinted within the seeker, serving as a touchstone for moments when they seek clarity, peace, or guidance.

After exploring these higher realms, the practitioner gently returns to their ordinary awareness by grounding the inner light back into the body. This grounding practice is essential, as it anchors the expanded awareness gained through meditation, integrating it into daily life. The practitioner visualizes the light returning to the heart center, breathing it gently through the body, feeling each part of themselves reawakening to the present moment. This grounding reinforces the connection between the divine and the physical, helping the seeker embody the wisdom and insights gained from the meditation in practical ways.

With each session, Inner Light Meditation becomes a powerful tool, transforming not only the meditation practice itself but the practitioner's entire experience of life. The light becomes a source of constant renewal, a companion that guides, heals, and protects. It brings clarity in moments of confusion, strength in moments of vulnerability, and wisdom in times of uncertainty. The inner light is no longer a distant concept but a living presence, a reminder of the divine within.

The seeker finds that, over time, this light becomes a guiding force, a source of spontaneous insight that aligns them with their highest purpose. The inner light offers a pathway to the mysteries of gnosis, leading the practitioner beyond the limits of the material and into a deeper understanding of their own essence and the divine reality that surrounds all. Through this expanded practice, the Gnostic seeker learns that the inner light is not only a part of themselves but a reflection of the infinite, a beacon that guides them on their path to unity with the Pleroma.

Chapter 14
Communication with the Higher Self

In the Gnostic journey, the Higher Self represents the purest aspect of the individual—a direct connection to divine wisdom and the Pleroma. This Higher Self, often described as the soul's truest voice, transcends the ordinary thoughts and ego-driven impulses of daily life. For the Gnostic seeker, learning to establish communication with this inner essence is fundamental to achieving self-knowledge and accessing deeper spiritual truths. This chapter explores the practices that foster a dialogue with the Higher Self, allowing the practitioner to align their actions and choices with higher guidance.

The practice of communicating with the Higher Self begins with quieting the mind, creating a space within that can receive insight without interference from daily thoughts or emotions. The practitioner finds a calm, quiet place, free from distractions, and settles into a meditative posture. Breathing deeply, they allow each inhale and exhale to bring them deeper into relaxation, releasing tension and clearing away mental noise. With each breath, the mind grows quieter, more still, until it reaches a receptive, open state—one in which the subtle presence of the Higher Self can be sensed.

Once this state of quietude is achieved, the seeker shifts their awareness inward, focusing on the heart center or a place within that resonates with peace and clarity. The practitioner gently invites the presence of the Higher Self, acknowledging it as an inner guide. This invitation is not a command or forceful request; rather, it is a gesture of openness, a silent recognition of the Higher Self's presence. The seeker sits with this awareness, feeling a subtle shift within, a sensation of warmth, calm, or gentle clarity that signals the presence of the Higher Self.

As this connection deepens, the practitioner may experience a sense of inner dialogue, a quiet, intuitive flow of thoughts or feelings that seem to arise from a place beyond the ordinary mind. These impressions are often subtle, requiring patience and sensitivity to recognize. The seeker learns to differentiate this inner voice from everyday mental chatter by observing its qualities—the guidance from the Higher Self is calm, wise, and compassionate, carrying a sense of clarity without judgment. This voice may appear as a feeling, an image, or a simple word, yet it resonates deeply within, often sparking a feeling of recognition or truth.

To strengthen this connection, the practitioner may use a simple question-and-answer technique, a gentle inquiry posed inwardly to the Higher Self. For example, the seeker might ask, "What guidance do I need today?" or "What is the next step on my spiritual path?" After asking, they sit in receptive silence, allowing any response to emerge naturally. These responses often arrive not as direct answers but as symbols, impressions, or subtle insights. The practitioner trusts whatever arises, knowing that, even if it feels ambiguous at first, the message will reveal itself with time and reflection.

For some, keeping a journal dedicated to insights from the Higher Self can be a powerful tool. After each meditation or moment of connection, the seeker writes down impressions, thoughts, or feelings that arose, capturing the nuances of the experience. This journal serves as a sacred space where the practitioner can revisit the guidance received, noticing patterns, themes, or recurring messages over time. Through journaling, the seeker learns to trust the Higher Self, seeing how each message builds upon previous ones, weaving a larger tapestry of insight and guidance.

Another technique involves working with a symbolic representation of the Higher Self, such as an image, a candle, or a small object that embodies qualities like wisdom or purity. This symbol becomes a focal point, a visual reminder of the Higher Self's presence. The practitioner places this object on an altar or in their meditation space, sitting with it before beginning their meditation. Focusing on this symbol, they allow it to guide them into a state of openness, as if it were a doorway leading to the inner realms where the Higher Self resides. Through repeated practice, this symbol grows powerful, becoming a bridge to the inner voice.

An essential aspect of communicating with the Higher Self is learning to distinguish its guidance from the impulses of the ego. The Higher Self speaks with a sense of calm certainty, free from urgency, anxiety, or self-interest. In contrast, ego-based impulses often carry a sense of urgency, fear, or a desire for validation. By observing these differences, the seeker learns to recognize and trust the subtle, compassionate voice of the Higher Self, allowing it to guide their choices and actions with clarity and inner peace.

In challenging moments, the practitioner can turn to the Higher Self for comfort and strength, especially when faced with decisions or experiences that provoke fear, doubt, or confusion. By connecting with the Higher Self in these times, the seeker finds a steadying presence, a reminder of their own inner wisdom. Through this connection, the practitioner becomes less reactive, learning to respond from a place of calm insight rather than impulsive emotion. This practice fosters resilience, helping the seeker remain grounded and clear, even in difficult situations.

Another useful exercise is visualizing the Higher Self as a radiant light above or within. During meditation, the practitioner imagines a luminous presence, a source of pure light that represents the highest aspects of their soul. They envision this light filling their entire being, gently guiding each thought and feeling into alignment with the divine. This visualization reinforces the sense of connection, making the Higher Self feel more tangible and present. As this light fills the seeker's awareness, they may experience a profound sense of unity and purpose, a recognition that they are in tune with a deeper truth.

Over time, communicating with the Higher Self becomes second nature, a subtle but constant presence that accompanies the seeker throughout their day. Whether in quiet reflection or in the midst of daily activity, the practitioner learns to listen inwardly, attuned to the Higher Self's guidance. This connection transforms the seeker's inner landscape, making each experience an opportunity for insight, growth, and alignment with their soul's purpose.

As the Gnostic practitioner strengthens this bond, the Higher Self becomes not just a guide but a mirror, reflecting the divine essence that resides within. The path becomes illuminated by this inner light, each step guided by a wisdom that transcends ordinary perception. This ongoing dialogue with the Higher Self opens doors to the mysteries of the soul, drawing the seeker ever closer to the truths hidden within and the divine fullness beyond. Through this communion, the practitioner comes to understand that the Higher Self is not a distant ideal but the truest, most authentic self—waiting, always, to guide them home.

As the Gnostic seeker grows accustomed to the subtle yet profound presence of the Higher Self, they now embark on a deeper journey into the practices that refine and expand this connection. This stage introduces advanced methods, such as automatic writing, guided meditation, and the art of inner surrender, all of which invite the Higher Self's voice into daily life and important decision-making. Through these practices, the seeker learns not only to receive insight but to embody the wisdom, compassion, and clarity of the Higher Self, transforming their inner landscape.

One powerful tool in deepening communication with the Higher Self is automatic writing, a meditative practice that allows messages from the Higher Self to flow freely onto the page. The practitioner begins by entering a quiet, relaxed state, focusing on the breath, and inviting the presence of the Higher Self. With a pen and paper or digital device at hand, the seeker sets an intention, asking a question or simply inviting guidance. In a calm, open state, they begin to write, letting thoughts, impressions, or even fragments of phrases flow without judgment or analysis. The words may appear fragmented or unclear at first, but as the practice continues, insights, patterns, and messages emerge that feel both intuitive and aligned with higher wisdom.

Automatic writing is not only a form of communication but also an exercise in trust and surrender, allowing the practitioner to release control and welcome the unknown. Over time, the seeker may notice recurring themes, symbols, or phrases that reflect deeper truths and offer gentle guidance on personal issues, spiritual questions, or life decisions. This practice helps the seeker recognize and trust the subtle voice of the Higher Self, building confidence in this inner guidance. The messages recorded in these sessions become a sacred archive, a written record of the soul's journey and the wisdom gained along the way.

In addition to automatic writing, the practitioner can use guided meditation to access the Higher Self in moments of need. This meditation often involves visualizing a sacred space, such as a garden, temple, or mountaintop, where the Higher Self appears as a figure of light or a symbolic presence. The seeker approaches this presence with reverence, asking a question or simply being open to receiving whatever guidance arises. In this visualization, the Higher Self may communicate through symbols, gestures, or even spoken words that resonate deeply within the practitioner's awareness. These meditative encounters often bring clarity, insight, and reassurance, reinforcing the Higher Self's role as a wise and compassionate guide.

As the practitioner becomes more attuned to the Higher Self's presence, they learn to integrate this connection into daily decision-making. Before responding to challenges or making choices, the seeker takes a quiet moment to ask, "How would my Higher Self respond to this?" In this brief pause, they invite the qualities of wisdom, patience, and clarity to inform their perspective. This shift in awareness often reveals unexpected insights, allowing the practitioner to approach each situation from a place of calm confidence. Over time, this habit of consulting the Higher Self fosters a greater sense of harmony, as each action becomes aligned with the soul's highest intentions.

A profound tool in advanced communication with the Higher Self is the practice of inner surrender, a state of deep openness in which the practitioner releases personal desires, fears, or attachments and invites the Higher Self to guide them. This practice involves letting go of expectations or specific outcomes, trusting that the Higher Self's wisdom will lead them toward what is truly needed for their spiritual growth. In moments of surrender, the practitioner may feel a sense of release, as if a weight has been lifted, allowing them to experience life with greater peace and flexibility. This surrender fosters a profound faith in the Higher Self, teaching the practitioner to navigate life's uncertainties with a heart open to divine guidance.

In the realm of Gnostic practice, dreamwork also becomes a path to connecting with the Higher Self. By setting an intention before sleep, the seeker invites the Higher Self to communicate through dreams. These dreams often hold symbolic meaning, revealing messages that resonate with the soul's inner questions or challenges. Upon waking, the practitioner records these dreams, reflecting on their symbols and themes to uncover the Higher Self's guidance hidden within. This dream practice can yield profound insights, as the language of the Higher Self is often conveyed through metaphor and symbol, speaking directly to the heart rather than the intellect.

Another powerful approach in this stage is the practice of deep listening, a form of meditation in which the practitioner sits quietly, focusing on the heart center, and simply listens for the Higher Self's guidance. This deep listening is a receptive state, free from expectation or effort, where the seeker allows any insights, images, or feelings to arise naturally. The voice of the Higher Self is often quiet, requiring patience and openness. Through regular practice, the seeker learns to attune to this subtle guidance, distinguishing it from the noise of daily thoughts and emotions.

For those moments when clarity is elusive, the practitioner can use a symbolic mirror exercise to reflect on the self and invite the Higher Self's insight. This exercise involves sitting in front of a physical mirror or visualizing oneself in a mirror within the mind's eye. The practitioner gazes into their own reflection, silently inviting the Higher Self to offer insight into their current state or specific challenges. Through this symbolic gaze, the practitioner begins to see themselves from a higher perspective, often noticing truths about their emotions, motivations, or fears that may have been hidden from ordinary awareness.

As the bond with the Higher Self strengthens, the practitioner experiences a shift in their inner world—a transformation marked by a deepening sense of self-compassion and acceptance. The seeker begins to recognize that the Higher Self's guidance is always compassionate, free from criticism or harsh judgment. This compassionate guidance becomes a model for how the practitioner relates to themselves, fostering self-acceptance, patience, and understanding. By embodying these qualities, the seeker aligns more closely with the Higher Self, making each moment a reflection of divine wisdom.

Ultimately, this ongoing dialogue with the Higher Self transforms the seeker's perception of themselves and the world around them. The Higher Self becomes not just a voice but a presence—a constant source of peace, clarity, and strength. With each interaction, the seeker feels a deeper alignment with their true essence, a sense of purpose and unity with the divine. This connection extends beyond moments of meditation or practice, becoming a living relationship that infuses daily life with meaning and direction.

In this advanced stage, the Gnostic seeker no longer views the Higher Self as something separate or distant; it is understood as the truest aspect of themselves, a guiding light that leads them toward the fullness of gnosis. Each practice, whether writing, meditating, or simply listening, becomes a step closer to integrating this higher wisdom into every aspect of life. Through this communion, the seeker finds that they are never alone, for the Higher Self is a faithful guide, always present, always illuminating the way forward on the journey to divine understanding.

Chapter 15
Symbolism of the Arcanum

The journey into Gnostic symbolism reveals a world rich with imagery, hidden meanings, and archetypal truths, embodied in what are often called the "arcanum." In Gnostic tradition, arcanum refers to symbolic elements that represent the mysteries of the inner self and the universe. Each symbol, whether it be an image, a number, or an abstract concept, acts as a gateway to higher knowledge, allowing the practitioner to access and understand truths that lie beyond the literal. This chapter begins the exploration of these symbols, teaching the practitioner to see beyond the surface and perceive the sacred insights they hold.

At the heart of Gnostic symbolism is the understanding that symbols are not mere representations but living expressions of divine truths. They speak to the soul in ways that words cannot, unlocking deep, often unconscious knowledge within. As the seeker begins to engage with these symbols, they are encouraged to approach them with reverence and openness, recognizing that each symbol has layers of meaning that reveal themselves gradually, according to the seeker's own readiness and understanding.

One of the primary symbols in Gnosticism is the serpent, an image that holds dual meanings across many spiritual traditions. In Gnostic thought, the serpent is not merely a representation of temptation or deception, as it is often depicted, but a symbol of knowledge and transformation. This interpretation comes from the belief that true wisdom often challenges established norms, pushing the seeker to question and transcend boundaries. As the practitioner meditates on the serpent, they are invited to consider their own path to wisdom, recognizing the times when seeking truth has required courage, discernment, and sometimes going against convention.

Another potent symbol is the lotus, which in Gnostic tradition represents purity and the unfolding of the soul. Emerging from mud yet blossoming into something beautiful, the lotus embodies the spiritual journey—how one's own growth can lead from darkness to light, from ignorance to enlightenment. When meditating on the lotus, the practitioner reflects on their journey, honoring both the struggles and the insights that have brought them to greater awareness. Through this symbol, the seeker recognizes the beauty inherent in transformation and the sacredness of their own path.

The number seven also carries powerful meaning within Gnostic symbolism, representing completion, mystery, and the layers of spiritual ascent. From the seven days of creation to the seven heavens in various mystical traditions, this number speaks to the journey from the material to the spiritual realms. In the Gnostic perspective, seven symbolizes the stages of awakening, where each level brings deeper insights and closer communion with the divine. The seeker may use the number seven as a framework for their own spiritual practice, viewing each day, each stage, as part of a divine unfolding.

As the practitioner explores these symbols, they are encouraged to deepen their understanding through active contemplation, focusing on a specific symbol and allowing it to reveal its meanings in layers. The seeker may begin by visualizing the symbol, holding it in their mind's eye while sitting in silence. By asking inwardly, "What does this symbol mean for me?" they invite a personal interpretation that goes beyond intellectual understanding. The insights gained through this contemplation are unique, arising from the practitioner's own experiences, dreams, and spiritual journey.

Another fundamental Gnostic symbol is the spiral, often seen as a representation of the soul's path—a journey that may seem circular, yet ultimately ascends. The spiral is a reminder that even as the seeker faces recurring challenges or lessons, they are continually moving closer to the divine. Reflecting on the spiral, the practitioner recognizes that growth is not always linear; it can loop back on itself, revisiting past themes with new understanding. This symbol encourages patience and trust, teaching that every step, no matter how small, is part of the journey toward gnosis.

The use of color in Gnostic symbolism also holds profound meaning. Colors such as gold, white, and blue are often associated with purity, wisdom, and divine knowledge. Gold, for example, represents the alchemical transformation of the soul, a process where the practitioner refines their character and perception, moving from base, ego-driven consciousness to a state of spiritual enlightenment. In meditation, the seeker might visualize themselves bathed in golden light, symbolizing their own journey toward illumination and inner truth.

Gnostic symbols also often include mythological figures, each embodying archetypal qualities and divine wisdom. Figures like Sophia, the embodiment of divine wisdom, offer an intimate understanding of the qualities that the practitioner seeks to cultivate. Sophia represents both the longing for knowledge and the experience of divine revelation. Meditating on Sophia allows the seeker to connect with their own desire for wisdom, acknowledging both the light and the shadow aspects of this journey. The seeker may ask themselves, "How does wisdom speak to me?" and listen for the response within.

The cross, though frequently associated with traditional religious contexts, holds unique meaning within Gnostic symbolism, representing the intersection between the material and spiritual realms. In Gnosticism, the cross is not solely a symbol of suffering or sacrifice but also of transcendence and union. It embodies the soul's journey from earthly attachments to divine communion, a process of integrating opposites—such as light and dark, ego and soul—into a unified whole. When contemplating the cross, the practitioner reflects on how they can transcend the dualities of life, finding peace and meaning in the balance between the material and spiritual aspects of existence.

To enhance the understanding of these symbols, the seeker can engage in symbolic journaling, a practice where they record their reflections, insights, and dreams related to each symbol they encounter. This journal becomes a personal record of the spiritual journey, documenting how each symbol evolves in meaning over time. By revisiting these entries, the practitioner can observe patterns and connections that reveal deeper truths about their path. This journaling practice not only reinforces understanding but also strengthens the bond between the seeker and the symbol, making each one a part of their own inner landscape.

As the practitioner delves deeper, they come to understand that Gnostic symbols are not fixed but are living symbols, evolving as the seeker's consciousness grows. Each encounter with a symbol reveals new layers, showing how the symbol's meaning adapts to meet the seeker's current understanding. This process reflects the infinite nature of divine wisdom—each truth leads to another, unfolding without end, much like the spiral path of the soul.

Through the exploration of Gnostic symbols, the practitioner is reminded that the outer world is a reflection of the inner, and that the language of symbols speaks directly to the heart. Each symbol becomes a key, unlocking insights that cannot be reached through reason alone. In time, the Gnostic seeker learns to see these symbols as guides and companions, allies in their journey to self-knowledge, illumination, and unity with the divine.

As they learn to engage with and interpret the arcanum, the practitioner finds themselves moving beyond the literal and into the realm of the transcendent, where each symbol becomes a mirror reflecting their own inner depths. Through this symbolic language, the mysteries of the Gnostic path unfold, inviting the seeker into a deeper relationship with the divine mysteries and the boundless wisdom of the soul.

Having established a foundation in the symbolism of the arcanum, the Gnostic seeker now explores how these symbols can be applied in meditation, visualization, and intuitive practices, each one offering a pathway to self-discovery and spiritual insight. This advanced engagement with the arcanum moves beyond contemplation, inviting the seeker to immerse themselves fully in the symbols as living forces within their spiritual journey. Through these practices, each symbol becomes a mirror, reflecting deeper aspects of the soul and revealing the hidden currents that shape the seeker's path to gnosis.

In this stage, the practitioner is introduced to guided meditations using symbols, where each arcanum is visualized and experienced as a portal to higher understanding. For example, the practitioner may meditate on the symbol of the key, an ancient Gnostic emblem of access to hidden knowledge. They imagine a luminous key appearing in their mind's eye, then visualize themselves holding it, feeling its weight and texture. The key becomes a conduit for insight, as they picture themselves unlocking a hidden door within, entering a sacred space where wisdom awaits. This visualization technique allows the symbol to work within the subconscious, revealing aspects of knowledge that might otherwise remain obscured by the rational mind.

Another potent practice is dream incubation, where the practitioner meditates on a specific symbol before sleep, inviting dreams to reveal its deeper meanings. They might choose the symbol of the chalice, a Gnostic emblem of divine receptivity and inner nourishment. As they drift into sleep, they hold this image in their awareness, focusing on the chalice as a vessel of divine wisdom. In the dream state, the symbol may appear transformed—perhaps filled with light or accompanied by images that speak directly to the soul. Upon waking, the practitioner reflects on the dream's symbols, recording insights that arise, as each one serves to deepen their understanding of how the chalice speaks to them personally.

Symbolic visualization can also be used to uncover unconscious patterns, helping the seeker to recognize internal blockages or shadows that may hinder spiritual growth. For example, the practitioner may visualize the labyrinth, a symbol of the soul's journey through complexity and illusion toward enlightenment. They imagine themselves standing at the entrance of this labyrinth, acknowledging that each twist and turn represents an aspect of their inner self. As they navigate through it, they encounter symbols representing fears, desires, or unresolved experiences, each offering insight and guidance. By visualizing this journey, the seeker learns to embrace their inner challenges as essential steps on the path, understanding that even the darkest corridors eventually lead to light.

In addition to meditation and visualization, intuitive readings with symbols allow the seeker to access the arcanum's guidance in a more spontaneous way. This practice involves selecting symbols randomly, perhaps from a set of cards or images that represent various Gnostic symbols. For example, if the practitioner draws the symbol of the flame, an emblem of transformation and purification, they reflect on what this symbol may signify in the context of their life. The flame may suggest a need to let go of attachments, clear away old patterns, or seek renewal. This approach enables the seeker to use the arcanum dynamically, seeing each symbol as a response to the specific questions or challenges they are facing in the present.

A powerful aspect of advanced symbolic practice is the use of mandalas, circular designs that incorporate various symbols into a unified whole. Mandalas are seen as reflections of cosmic harmony and the soul's structure. The practitioner may choose to create their own mandala, incorporating symbols that resonate with their journey, such as the serpent, the lotus, the cross, and the flame. By arranging these symbols in a circular design, they engage in an act of self-expression and discovery, reflecting on how each symbol represents a part of their path. This creative process opens a dialogue with the Higher Self, as each element finds its place within the whole, revealing a map of the soul's journey.

Another advanced practice involves contemplating pairs of symbols to explore the interplay between opposing or complementary forces within the self. For example, the practitioner might work with the sun and moon as symbols of active and receptive energies, balancing the conscious and unconscious aspects of the soul. They visualize these symbols as two points of light within, sensing how each influences their inner world. By meditating on these dualities, the seeker begins to understand how harmony is achieved not by suppressing one force in favor of the other, but by integrating both in a dynamic, balanced way.

The Gnostic seeker may also engage in symbolic rituals, where they incorporate chosen symbols into their physical environment to anchor insights and intentions. For instance, if working with the symbol of the eye, a representation of spiritual vision and inner awareness, the practitioner might place an image of an eye on their altar, lighting a candle beside it during meditation. This ritual serves as a focal point, a way to ground the symbol's energy in the physical world. As the flame burns, the practitioner reflects on their intention to see more clearly—both outwardly and within. These symbolic rituals act as living prayers, aligning the practitioner's inner world with the qualities each symbol embodies.

In this stage, the practitioner begins to recognize archetypal themes in their personal experiences, understanding that the arcanum are not abstract ideas but reflections of universal energies present in everyday life. For instance, the journey of the hero, a symbol of the soul's quest for truth and self-mastery, may reveal itself in the seeker's own struggles and triumphs. The practitioner learns to see themselves in these archetypal roles, realizing that each trial, insight, and moment of growth is part of the same cosmic story told through the symbols of the arcanum.

With continued practice, the seeker finds that each symbol has layers of meaning that shift as their awareness expands. A symbol like the chalice, once seen as a vessel of wisdom, may later appear as a symbol of inner stillness and receptivity. This evolving relationship reflects the practitioner's own growth, showing that symbols are living elements in the spiritual path, mirroring the soul's changing understanding. In time, each symbol becomes a friend and teacher, one that guides the practitioner through the subtle depths of self and the vast realms of spirit.

Ultimately, these practices reveal that the arcanum are not merely tools or images but sacred keys that open doors to the mysteries of the soul. Each symbol, each image, is an invitation to explore and embrace the divine facets within, guiding the practitioner toward a more profound relationship with their true essence and the boundless wisdom of the Pleroma. As the seeker works with these symbols, they come to understand that the spiritual journey is not linear but cyclical, spiraling ever deeper into the infinite layers of gnosis.

Through this intimate engagement with the arcanum, the Gnostic seeker gains a language for the soul, a way to express and understand the profound truths that lie beyond words. The symbols become markers of the path, guiding each step with clarity and purpose. In time, the seeker discovers that each symbol, each arcanum, is not a separate entity but a reflection of the divine whole—a mirror through which the soul can see itself, ever expanding, ever seeking, and ever returning to the light.

Chapter 16
Inner Alchemy

In Gnosticism, inner alchemy represents the profound process of transforming the self, much like the ancient art of alchemical transmutation that seeks to change base metals into gold. However, in the inner alchemy of the soul, the goal is not material transformation but the elevation of consciousness, refining the practitioner's being from ego-bound perception to enlightened understanding. This alchemical path takes the seeker through stages of purification and spiritual refinement, awakening them to the hidden aspects of their nature and the divine potential within.

The process begins with understanding the nature of inner alchemy, which holds that each individual is composed of energies and qualities that can be refined and elevated. The elements that make up the inner self—emotions, thoughts, desires, and aspirations—are seen as raw materials. Through Gnostic practices, the seeker learns to recognize, purify, and harmonize these aspects, allowing them to align with the higher self. Inner alchemy teaches that true transformation occurs within and that the seeker's journey is to harness their own energies toward the divine essence of the soul.

The first step in inner alchemy is purification, a process of cleansing the self of thoughts, attachments, and patterns that obstruct spiritual clarity. The practitioner begins by examining their inner landscape, identifying emotions or beliefs that cloud their perception or keep them bound to fear and desire. Through self-reflective practices, they observe these tendencies with patience and compassion, bringing awareness to areas of resistance or imbalance. Purification involves meditative practices, where the seeker envisions these impurities dissolving like mist, leaving only the essence of their higher self to guide them forward.

One essential tool in this alchemical transformation is the element of fire, which represents purification, illumination, and spiritual energy. In meditation, the practitioner visualizes a flame within—perhaps in the heart or the center of the mind—allowing it to burn away impurities and reveal the clarity within. This inner fire does not consume but instead transforms, like a gentle furnace that refines the soul. The flame is not only a symbol but an active element in inner alchemy, a catalyst for the transmutation of lower energies into wisdom, courage, and compassion.

Another vital aspect of inner alchemy is working with breath as a conduit for energy and transformation. The breath is seen as both life force and spirit, a bridge between body and soul. The seeker practices focused breathing exercises to draw in positive energy, exhaling negativity and mental fog. With each breath, they visualize themselves becoming lighter, more centered, and more attuned to their inner being. Breathwork becomes a practice of nourishing the soul, infusing it with clarity and balance, allowing the practitioner to feel the energies within shift and harmonize.

To further the process of inner transformation, the practitioner learns the concept of spiritual distillation, a method of refining emotions and intentions. This process encourages the seeker to look at each feeling, desire, or impulse and examine its source and purpose. For example, feelings of anger or jealousy are observed not as obstacles but as opportunities for insight. By asking, "What is the root of this feeling?" or "How can this energy be redirected toward growth?" the practitioner distills the essence of each emotion, extracting understanding from every experience. This distilled essence becomes a powerful source of inner wisdom, guiding the practitioner to a place of balance and inner peace.

An essential stage in inner alchemy is transmutation, the conscious transformation of raw emotional energy into enlightened qualities. Here, emotions such as fear, doubt, and resentment are recognized as energies that, when harnessed correctly, can be transformed into qualities like courage, trust, and forgiveness. The practitioner visualizes these energies as forms or colors within their being, seeing them change, elevate, and harmonize. In transmutation, anger becomes clarity, fear becomes strength, and doubt becomes faith. Through this alchemical process, the practitioner experiences the power of transformation, seeing firsthand that their inner world is both malleable and divine.

Another profound practice in inner alchemy is meditative grounding, where the seeker visualizes themselves as rooted in both the material and spiritual worlds, like a tree with deep roots and branches reaching upward. This grounding practice helps the practitioner stay balanced, recognizing that true transformation does not mean escaping the physical world but fully integrating both physical and spiritual dimensions. As they visualize their roots drawing strength from the earth and their branches reaching toward the divine, they embody the principle of unity, balancing earthly existence with the soul's ascent.

As the seeker deepens in inner alchemy, they come to understand the role of the will in shaping their transformation. In Gnostic practice, the will is seen as a guiding force, a conscious choice to align actions, thoughts, and feelings with the soul's purpose. The practitioner learns to direct their will with intention, bringing it to every thought, every interaction, and every meditation. The cultivation of will becomes a sacred act, a dedication to the path of gnosis and a commitment to allow the divine spark within to guide every step.

Through inner alchemy, the seeker experiences the unveiling of the divine within, the true self that is both a part of them and beyond them. They come to realize that the purpose of transformation is not to become someone new, but to reveal the essence of who they truly are. The journey of inner alchemy is one of uncovering this divine essence, stripping away the layers of ego, doubt, and illusion until only the luminous self remains. The seeker experiences moments of deep recognition, glimpses of the eternal within themselves, and an understanding that all aspects of their being—physical, mental, emotional, and spiritual—are integral parts of the sacred whole.

In these moments of recognition, the practitioner sees their life as an alchemical vessel, a sacred space where transformation unfolds continuously. Every thought, action, and experience becomes an ingredient in the divine process, each one serving to elevate the soul closer to gnosis. Through the lens of inner alchemy, challenges are seen not as obstacles but as catalysts, each one an opportunity to refine, expand, and align with the true self.

This stage of inner alchemy is a path of humility and dedication, where the practitioner understands that transformation is both a gift and a responsibility. The inner light that is cultivated through this process is not only for personal enlightenment but also a source of guidance and compassion that radiates outward, touching others on their paths. In this way, the work of inner alchemy becomes an act of service, a dedication not only to self-realization but to the uplifting of all beings.

The journey of inner alchemy, therefore, is both an individual path and a universal one, a process that brings the practitioner into harmony with the Pleroma, the divine fullness that is present in all things. Through inner alchemy, the seeker transforms not only themselves but their experience of the world, seeing each moment, each interaction, and each breath as a step on the path to unity with the divine essence. The alchemical journey leads them ever deeper, into the mystery of their own soul and into the boundless light of gnosis.

In this advanced stage of inner alchemy, the Gnostic seeker is guided through deeper practices of transmutation, emotional refinement, and the elevation of vital energies to transform the self. Building upon the initial insights into inner purification, this phase delves into techniques for cultivating harmony and spiritual ascent, revealing how each element of consciousness can be refined into its highest form. By engaging with these practices, the practitioner embarks on a journey toward enlightenment, transcending egoic limitations and cultivating a profound inner radiance.

One of the core practices in this advanced stage is emotional transmutation, a process that teaches the seeker to transform dense or challenging emotions into refined, empowering qualities. Instead of suppressing or avoiding difficult feelings, the practitioner embraces them as energies to be redirected. For example, feelings of anger or frustration are seen as raw energies that, with mindful attention, can be transformed into clarity, strength, and determination. To achieve this, the practitioner brings awareness to the source of the emotion, allowing it to surface fully. Through focused breathing, they visualize this emotion moving upward, turning into light, transforming from a reaction into a consciously directed energy that can be used in spiritual practice.

Breathwork also takes on a more central role in this phase, particularly through advanced techniques designed to channel and elevate energy. The practitioner may engage in deep, rhythmic breathing, visualizing each breath as a wave of light that circulates through the body, purifying and revitalizing. As they inhale, they visualize pulling in positive, life-giving energy, and as they exhale, they imagine releasing any energies that do not serve their spiritual path. This process clears and refines the subtle channels within the body, making it receptive to higher energies. The breath becomes an alchemical force, allowing the practitioner to feel both grounded in the physical and expanded in spirit.

In this stage, sexual energy transmutation is introduced as a practice that holds significant transformative power. In Gnostic teachings, sexual energy is seen as a potent life force capable of fueling spiritual elevation. The practitioner learns to cultivate this energy not through repression but through mindful redirection, allowing it to become a source of vitality and insight. Through focused breathwork and visualization, they channel this energy from the lower centers of the body upward, raising it to the heart or mind centers. This act of sublimation awakens creative and spiritual energies, enhancing focus, intuition, and inner strength. The seeker understands that, when directed with conscious intent, this energy becomes a powerful ally in the journey toward enlightenment.

Alchemical visualization further enhances the transformative work, where the practitioner visualizes themselves as a vessel of light, in which raw energies are distilled and elevated. In meditation, they imagine themselves surrounded by an aura of radiant white or golden light. They picture any discordant energies within dissolving in this light, leaving only purified, harmonious energy. This visualization becomes a ritual of renewal, as the practitioner sees themselves transmuted, each element within—thoughts, emotions, physical sensations—rising to its highest form. The light they cultivate becomes a shield, a source of inner peace and strength that they can carry into every aspect of life.

The practitioner also begins to work with mantras and sacred sounds that resonate with the process of inner transformation. Mantras are repeated with deep focus, each sound carrying specific vibrational qualities that cleanse, balance, and elevate. The Gnostic seeker may chant these sacred sounds aloud or repeat them silently, feeling their resonance shift the energies within. These mantras are often associated with aspects of the divine, aligning the practitioner's inner energies with higher spiritual frequencies. Through this practice, the body, mind, and soul begin to resonate as a single, harmonious field, connected to the divine source.

A pivotal part of this stage is developing the ability to hold paradox, which is the Gnostic understanding that true spiritual growth often embraces apparent opposites. The practitioner learns to balance the light and dark within themselves, accepting that both are essential aspects of the soul's journey. This inner acceptance is not passive but an active choice to recognize and integrate all aspects of self, seeing each one as a necessary element in the alchemical process. The seeker learns that by acknowledging both the strengths and shadows within, they can create a complete, unified self that holds the depth and mystery of existence.

As the seeker progresses, the concept of the inner elixir becomes central. This elixir is a metaphor for the distilled essence of wisdom, love, and strength that is cultivated through inner alchemy. The practitioner visualizes this elixir within, perhaps as a radiant drop of liquid light in the heart center. Through meditation, they see this elixir spreading throughout their being, filling every cell, every thought, and every emotion with its transformative power. This inner elixir represents the culmination of their efforts, a concentrated essence of divine qualities that grows with each practice. The seeker learns that by nurturing this inner elixir, they can access wisdom, compassion, and clarity even in the midst of life's challenges.

Another powerful tool in this phase is mirror meditation, a practice that involves facing one's own reflection to recognize both the outer and inner self. The practitioner sits in front of a mirror and gazes into their own eyes, using the reflection as a portal to access deeper self-awareness. As they look into their own gaze, they hold a gentle focus, allowing any judgments or criticisms to dissolve, replaced by a sense of acceptance and love. In time, this practice reveals the divine spark within, helping the seeker to see past surface appearances and recognize their own essence as a being of light and wisdom. This practice reinforces the understanding that true transformation is not about becoming something else but about uncovering what was always within.

In the final stages of advanced inner alchemy, the seeker learns the practice of radiating their inner light outward. This act of spiritual service is seen as the highest form of transformation, where the inner alchemical process becomes a source of light for others. Through meditation, the practitioner visualizes their aura expanding, radiating peace, love, and wisdom into the world. This light is not only for themselves but is dedicated to all beings, with the intention of uplifting and healing. This practice brings the alchemical journey full circle, reminding the seeker that personal transformation contributes to the collective elevation of consciousness.

Through the continuous practice of inner alchemy, the practitioner becomes a living vessel of the divine, embodying a harmony that can be felt by others. The journey of inner alchemy is one of humility, self-dedication, and profound joy, as the seeker comes to know themselves not as separate or flawed, but as a radiant expression of the divine fullness. This realization is the ultimate aim of inner alchemy—a transformation that reveals the timeless truth that the light they sought was always within, waiting to be discovered and shared.

In the end, the alchemical journey does not reach a fixed destination but continues infinitely, with each moment, each breath, and each interaction offering an opportunity for further refinement and illumination. The Gnostic seeker comes to live this truth, carrying the elixir of wisdom and compassion within, forever walking the path of inner transmutation, ever in communion with the divine essence that resides in all things.

Chapter 17
Dream Work

In the Gnostic path, dreams are sacred doorways that reveal hidden realms of knowledge and self-understanding. These nightly visions are seen as messages from the depths of the soul, offering insights that are often obscured in the waking world. For the Gnostic practitioner, dream work is not a passive experience but a conscious practice—a path that opens new dimensions of awareness, allowing them to access personal and spiritual truths that enrich their journey of gnosis.

The first step in dream work is to cultivate dream recall, a skill that allows the seeker to remember and document their dreams in detail. This practice begins with setting a clear intention before sleep, a silent vow to recall dreams upon waking. By holding this intention, the practitioner activates a deeper awareness that stays present even as they sleep. Upon waking, they capture every image, color, or sensation they remember, noting even the smallest details in a dream journal kept close to their bed. This journal becomes a vital tool for the seeker, a living archive of the soul's messages, allowing them to observe recurring themes and symbols over time.

As the practitioner begins to remember their dreams more vividly, they start the practice of interpreting dream symbols, seeing them as elements of the inner world that communicate through metaphor. In the Gnostic tradition, dream symbols are not simply random; they carry meanings that connect to both the personal and the spiritual self. For example, a house in a dream might represent the structure of one's inner life, with each room symbolizing an aspect of the self or a memory. Water often represents emotion, flow, and the subconscious, while mountains can symbolize spiritual goals or challenges. By interpreting these symbols, the practitioner unveils layers of meaning within themselves, observing how each symbol mirrors their current state of consciousness.

A powerful technique in dream work is asking questions before sleep, a practice known as dream incubation. The seeker meditates on a question or challenge, holding it gently in their awareness before drifting into sleep. They might ask for guidance on a decision, clarity about an emotional struggle, or insight into a recurring pattern. This question acts as a beacon, inviting the subconscious mind to respond with symbols, images, or scenarios in the dream state. Upon waking, they reflect on how the dream's symbols relate to their question, often finding subtle yet profound answers that were inaccessible to the conscious mind.

Lucid dreaming is another potent practice, allowing the seeker to remain aware and even exercise choice within their dreams. This practice requires patience and intent, beginning with the habit of "reality checking" throughout the day—asking oneself, "Am I dreaming?" This habit eventually carries over into the dream state, enabling the practitioner to become aware within the dream. Once lucid, they can explore the dream landscape consciously, seeking wisdom, interacting with symbols, or simply observing the depths of their subconscious with clarity. Lucid dreams become a dynamic field of exploration, where the seeker can confront fears, receive guidance, and experience the fluid nature of reality itself.

A foundational aspect of Gnostic dream work is recognizing and integrating the shadow, those hidden parts of oneself that often surface in dreams as symbols of fear, conflict, or mystery. The shadow represents the unacknowledged aspects of the self, such as suppressed emotions, unresolved memories, or unexpressed desires. In dreams, these aspects may appear as dark figures, turbulent waters, or unknown landscapes. By acknowledging and embracing these symbols, the seeker brings these hidden parts into the light, transforming what was once feared into an integrated part of their being. This process of shadow work leads to self-acceptance, inner harmony, and a clearer understanding of the soul's wholeness.

In Gnostic tradition, archetypal symbols often appear in dreams, representing universal themes that transcend individual experience. Figures such as the wise sage, the inner child, or the guardian often emerge, offering guidance and companionship on the inner journey. The sage, for instance, may appear in the form of a teacher or elder, providing insight that resonates deeply with the seeker's spiritual questions. The inner child symbolizes innocence and intuition, reminding the practitioner of the purity within, while guardians offer protection and courage during challenging moments. These archetypal encounters bring a sense of reverence to the dreamscape, as the practitioner recognizes these figures as timeless forces guiding their journey toward self-realization.

Recording recurring themes in dreams also reveals profound insights, as patterns often reflect underlying concerns or desires. For example, dreams of searching, flying, or confronting barriers might signal areas where the practitioner seeks growth, liberation, or resolution. By observing these recurring themes, the practitioner discerns their soul's current focus, understanding where attention and healing are needed. These patterns are seen as messages from the deeper self, indicating the areas in which the seeker is ready for transformation and integration.

A crucial element in dream work is the practice of non-attachment, where the practitioner learns to observe dreams without becoming entangled in emotional responses. In this practice, the seeker views each dream as a piece of the inner puzzle, a reflection of shifting energies and insights. Rather than becoming fixated on intense emotions or disturbing images, they approach each dream with curiosity and compassion, understanding that each symbol, no matter how challenging, carries wisdom for the journey. This attitude of detachment allows the practitioner to move through their dreams with ease, extracting lessons without becoming caught in emotional loops.

Over time, the practitioner may notice that their dreams begin to connect with waking life, weaving symbols and messages that appear in both states of consciousness. A symbol encountered in a dream may appear later in daily life, deepening its significance. This synchronicity is seen as a form of spiritual guidance, a reminder that the boundaries between the waking and dream worlds are fluid and that wisdom flows continuously from one realm to the other. The practitioner learns to recognize these signs, trusting that their inner guidance is always present, both in dreams and in waking life.

As dream work progresses, dreams often become a source of healing, bringing to light unresolved feelings and memories that require attention. The practitioner might experience dreams where they revisit past experiences or encounter figures from their past. In these dreams, they have the opportunity to engage in healing dialogues, offering forgiveness or understanding where it was previously lacking. This dream healing is a gift from the subconscious, a chance to resolve inner tensions and liberate the soul from attachments to past wounds.

Dream work ultimately becomes a way of life, a sacred practice that extends beyond the hours of sleep. The practitioner sees each night as a journey, an opportunity to reconnect with the inner self, to explore realms of wisdom, and to bring the insights of the soul into waking life. As they deepen in this practice, they develop a profound trust in their own inner guidance, knowing that the soul speaks through dreams, offering wisdom, healing, and companionship on the Gnostic path.

Through this practice, the Gnostic seeker learns that the dream world is not separate from their spiritual journey but an integral part of it. Each dream becomes a bridge, connecting the depths of the soul to the divine mysteries beyond, guiding the practitioner in their continuous journey toward self-knowledge, transformation, and inner peace.

With a foundational understanding of dream work, the Gnostic seeker now moves into advanced practices that deepen their engagement with the dream state, using it as a direct conduit for spiritual insight and communication with realms beyond the ordinary mind. This phase of dream work guides the practitioner toward lucid encounters, purposeful interaction with spiritual guides, and techniques for exploring layers of consciousness that extend far into the mysteries of gnosis. Here, dreams become a sacred landscape, a place where the practitioner can actively access hidden knowledge and experience dimensions of the soul and the cosmos.

At this advanced level, the seeker practices lucid dream induction with intention, where they set a specific goal before sleep, aiming not only to achieve lucidity but to explore a particular theme or seek a direct answer from the dream state. By cultivating this intention with focused visualization and affirmation, the seeker "prepares" their consciousness, setting the stage to recognize the dream as it unfolds. When lucidity arises, they move forward with their intended purpose, whether it be seeking guidance, interacting with a symbolic figure, or traveling to a particular place in the dream world. Each lucid experience becomes a bridge to realms of insight, often unveiling spiritual dimensions of existence that might be inaccessible during ordinary waking consciousness.

Engaging with spiritual guides in the dream world becomes a central practice at this stage. Spiritual guides—sometimes appearing as familiar or archetypal figures—offer wisdom, support, and instruction that resonate with the soul's deepest aspirations. The seeker may encounter a figure who speaks with profound clarity, conveying messages that stay with them long after waking. These guides often appear unbidden, yet the practitioner can also call upon them consciously within the dream. By developing a relationship with these guides, the seeker finds a trusted source of insight that complements their inner journey, drawing on the vast well of universal wisdom that dreams offer.

Another advanced practice involves using dream symbols for self-activation, where specific symbols serve as anchors, activating certain qualities or insights within the seeker. For example, a symbol like a mountain, a tree, or a star might hold personal or spiritual significance, representing strength, rootedness, or guidance. The practitioner visualizes encountering this symbol in the dream, using it as a touchstone that triggers recognition of these qualities within themselves. Over time, these symbols become powerful allies, easily accessed during waking meditation or in moments of need, allowing the seeker to summon the dream's energy into everyday life.

Exploring the astral plane through dream work offers yet another layer of spiritual discovery, as the seeker learns to traverse dimensions that reveal universal mysteries. The astral plane is often perceived as a realm of spiritual significance, a place where the soul can transcend physical boundaries and experience a direct connection to the divine. When lucid, the practitioner may find themselves floating or moving without limitation, journeying through places that feel ancient, timeless, or unearthly. These dream journeys offer profound understanding of the interconnectedness of all existence, as well as a sense of unity with the cosmic order. The seeker comes to appreciate that the astral plane is not separate from them but an intrinsic part of their expanded spiritual awareness.

Healing through dream re-entry becomes an essential part of this stage, where the practitioner returns to a particular dream to resolve unresolved elements, integrate insights, or bring healing to a troubling or fragmented scene. To practice dream re-entry, the seeker recalls the dream vividly, entering a relaxed state and envisioning themselves back within it, interacting with its symbols or characters to alter the experience. If they had experienced fear, they might return with the intention to face that fear, transforming it into strength. This act of conscious re-engagement allows them to shift their inner response to the dream's symbols, freeing themselves from recurring themes and releasing subconscious blockages.

Another powerful aspect of advanced dream work is the practice of receiving spiritual messages, where the practitioner sets the intention to receive guidance from a higher source. This might take the form of words, visions, or symbols that appear with profound clarity. Often, the messages convey truths that resonate deeply with the soul, affirming the seeker's path or providing clarity on an unresolved question. These messages are seen as gifts from the divine, offering wisdom and encouragement on the Gnostic path. The practitioner learns to approach this experience with humility, recognizing that dreams carry truths that can guide them through both their spiritual and daily lives.

Dream healing for others is an extension of the seeker's practice, where they consciously send intentions of peace, love, or protection to those in need. Before sleep, the practitioner holds a vision of the person they wish to assist, seeing them surrounded by light or calm energy. In the dream, they might encounter this individual, offering supportive words, images, or simply the warmth of their presence. This act of dream-based service is a form of spiritual compassion, affirming that dreams are not only tools for personal insight but also a way to channel healing energies to those beyond oneself. The practitioner feels the interconnectedness of all beings, understanding that through dreams, they can contribute to the well-being of others.

In this advanced phase, the seeker also develops the ability to observe collective symbols and archetypes that appear in dreams, recognizing how their personal experience reflects universal themes shared by humanity. They may dream of events, symbols, or figures that seem to resonate with collective energies, revealing aspects of the human journey such as creation, destruction, renewal, and redemption. By engaging with these archetypes, the practitioner connects with the broader spiritual landscape, understanding their own journey as part of the collective evolution of consciousness.

One of the most profound experiences in this phase is the realization of shared dreams or encounters with other conscious dreamers on the Gnostic path. Sometimes, the practitioner may find themselves in a shared space with familiar figures, perhaps even experiencing conversations or scenes that feel as real as waking life. This shared experience is understood as a meeting of souls, a recognition that all seekers are ultimately united in their quest for truth and self-knowledge. Through these shared dreams, the practitioner senses that consciousness transcends individual experience, connecting each soul in a vast, divine network.

As the Gnostic seeker reaches a deeper understanding of dream work, they begin to see that dreams reflect the soul's continuous journey, a process of unfolding wisdom and growth that neither begins nor ends with waking or sleep. Every dream becomes a piece of the divine puzzle, a glimpse into the nature of existence and the limitless depths of the self. This practice brings a sense of reverence, as the seeker recognizes dreams as a sacred expression of their evolving consciousness.

In these moments of dream-induced insight, the practitioner understands that the ultimate purpose of dream work is not simply to find answers but to cultivate a state of awakened presence that bridges all states of being. The dream world becomes a luminous part of their spiritual path, a realm where they can encounter the infinite, access divine knowledge, and experience the boundless potential of the soul. Through dream work, the Gnostic seeker walks a path that leads beyond dreams, into the heart of gnosis, ever deepening their connection to the divine mysteries.

Chapter 18
Connection with Spiritual Entities

In the Gnostic journey, the presence of spiritual entities—beings that dwell within realms beyond the material world—serves as a profound source of insight, protection, and companionship. These entities, ranging from guardian spirits to guides and angelic forces, are considered allies on the path to self-knowledge, existing within realms that intersect with human consciousness. The practice of connecting with these entities is not undertaken lightly; it requires respect, purity of intention, and an open heart willing to listen to the subtle language of spirit.

The first step in establishing this sacred connection is cultivating awareness of spiritual presence. The practitioner begins by developing sensitivity to energies within and around them. This awareness is often cultivated through meditation, where the seeker focuses on subtle sensations, feelings, or shifts in the energy of their surroundings. By entering a quiet, receptive state, they may sense a comforting warmth, a tingling sensation, or an inexplicable presence that feels both gentle and strong. This practice of attunement allows the practitioner to perceive the difference between their personal energy and that of other spiritual beings.

With heightened awareness, the next step is setting a clear intention for connection. Spiritual entities respond most openly when the practitioner approaches with a genuine desire for learning and growth rather than curiosity alone. The seeker begins by meditating on their intention, perhaps asking for guidance, support, or protection. By expressing gratitude and respect for the entity they wish to connect with, the practitioner invites a benevolent presence into their experience. This clear intention not only attracts positive energies but also ensures that the connection is grounded in integrity and mutual respect.

Creating a sacred space enhances this connection further, providing a safe environment that aligns with higher energies. The practitioner may prepare a quiet area, lighting candles or incense, placing meaningful symbols or objects on an altar, or playing soft, meditative music to elevate the space's vibration. The act of preparing this space is itself a form of invocation, signaling an openness to communion with the spiritual realm. This sacred space serves as a gateway, a place where the boundaries between the physical and spiritual worlds become more fluid, allowing for a deeper experience.

In this stage, invocation practices are introduced, teaching the practitioner how to formally call upon spiritual entities. Invocation involves using specific words, visualizations, or symbols to summon a particular type of entity, such as a guardian angel, an ancestor, or a guide aligned with the seeker's path. These words may be spoken aloud or repeated silently, with the practitioner visualizing the desired entity in the form of light, a symbol, or even a subtle presence. This practice invites the entity into the space with respect, acknowledging its higher wisdom and the sacredness of the interaction. The seeker remains in a receptive state, allowing their mind to quiet and their heart to open, ready to listen.

The practice of asking for signs is also valuable in initial connections, as spiritual entities often communicate through symbols, sensations, or impressions that might seem subtle yet carry significant meaning. The practitioner may ask for a sign, such as a particular image, word, or sensation, to confirm the presence of a spiritual guide. Signs may appear in different forms—a sudden sense of peace, an intuitive flash, or even a synchronistic event in the days that follow. By remaining attentive, the seeker learns to recognize the distinct "language" of the entity, building a bridge of communication that transcends words.

In building this relationship, the Gnostic seeker must also cultivate discernment, understanding that not all spiritual presences are beneficial. The practitioner learns to trust their intuition, sensing whether an energy is uplifting or if it brings tension or discomfort. A feeling of warmth, calm, or inspiration generally indicates a benevolent presence, while feelings of unease suggest that the practitioner should politely disengage and return to their personal energy. Over time, the seeker becomes adept at discerning, guided by their inner wisdom and a commitment to staying aligned with entities that serve their highest good.

The practice of energy grounding becomes essential in interactions with spiritual entities, helping the practitioner remain balanced and connected to their physical body. After invoking or connecting with an entity, the seeker grounds themselves by focusing on the breath, visualizing roots extending from their feet into the earth, or feeling the weight of their body. This practice stabilizes their energy, preventing them from feeling disoriented or "too open" after the interaction. Grounding reaffirms the practitioner's presence within the physical world, ensuring they maintain balance as they explore the spiritual dimensions.

As the practitioner deepens their connection, they may experience messages from entities, often received as impressions, insights, or even brief phrases that come to mind without conscious thought. These messages may feel like spontaneous realizations, clear and resonant with a wisdom beyond ordinary thought. To deepen this communication, the practitioner keeps a journal, recording impressions and reflections that arise during or after interactions. This journal becomes a record of their spiritual conversations, revealing patterns, guidance, and the evolution of the relationship over time.

At this stage, the practitioner might also encounter guardian entities, protectors that watch over them and guide them through challenges on the Gnostic path. Guardians often appear during difficult times, providing comfort or a sense of safety that allows the seeker to navigate challenges with resilience. To connect with a guardian, the practitioner can engage in a simple invocation, asking for protection and guidance. They might visualize themselves surrounded by a sphere of light, feeling the presence of a protective force around them. This relationship becomes a source of strength, reminding the seeker that they are never alone on the path.

For the Gnostic practitioner, connecting with spiritual entities also serves as an act of humility and reverence, a reminder that wisdom exists in countless forms beyond human experience. By acknowledging the presence of these beings, the seeker cultivates a sense of respect for the mysteries of existence, understanding that spiritual entities, too, are on their own journey of service and evolution. This respect brings a profound sense of unity, an awareness that all beings—seen and unseen—are interconnected within the divine fabric of creation.

The connection with spiritual entities also encourages the practitioner to expand their understanding of self, recognizing that consciousness is not limited to physical experience but extends into multiple dimensions. Each interaction with an entity broadens the seeker's awareness, challenging them to let go of rigid ideas about reality and embrace the vast, dynamic nature of existence. In time, the practitioner understands that the self is fluid, capable of connecting across realms, and that each encounter is a reflection of their own expanding consciousness.

Through these practices, the Gnostic seeker gradually forms a sacred bond with the spiritual entities that guide, protect, and teach along the path to gnosis. These connections become an integral part of the practitioner's spiritual life, offering companionship and guidance as they delve into the mysteries of existence and the depths of self. Each encounter strengthens their inner resolve, serving as a reminder of the boundless wisdom that surrounds them and the divine support available in their quest for truth.

This chapter on connecting with spiritual entities invites the seeker to experience a more profound relationship with the unseen, recognizing these presences as allies and teachers in their journey. Each step on this path of connection, from invocation to grounding, serves as an act of devotion, a journey into the heart of Gnostic practice where the veil between worlds grows thin and the mysteries of spirit unfold with every interaction.

As the Gnostic seeker deepens their connection with spiritual entities, this advanced stage offers techniques for profound interaction, discernment, and integration of spiritual guidance into daily life. Here, the practitioner engages in practices that refine the ability to invoke, converse with, and honor entities from realms beyond the physical, understanding that each interaction is a step toward unity with the divine.

One of the core practices in this phase is invocation through sacred ritual. By establishing a formalized ritual, the practitioner sets a powerful framework for communicating with spiritual entities. Ritual elements, such as lighting candles, reciting invocations, or creating symbolic offerings, serve as a bridge, signaling a respectful request for presence. Each component of the ritual reflects the qualities the seeker wishes to invite into their space—light for clarity, incense for purification, water for emotional insight. This ritual process honors the sacredness of the exchange, reinforcing the boundaries and intentions of the practice.

Establishing boundaries with entities becomes crucial at this level, as it allows the practitioner to set clear terms for interaction. With increasing sensitivity, the seeker may find that spiritual entities make their presence known unexpectedly, sometimes at inopportune moments. By establishing boundaries—stating a preference for connection during specific times or within certain spaces—the practitioner ensures that their experiences remain balanced and respectful. This is achieved through a firm yet respectful declaration of intent, where the practitioner asserts their desire to connect only when the timing and conditions are conducive to their spiritual well-being.

The practice of discernment takes on even greater importance in advanced connection work. Discernment is not only about sensing the presence of benevolent entities but also understanding the purpose and message of each encounter. The practitioner must rely on intuition and inner wisdom, asking themselves questions such as, "Does this presence bring peace and clarity?" or "Is this message consistent with my spiritual growth?" If an entity or message brings confusion or fear, the practitioner calmly disengages, using grounding techniques or visualizing a protective sphere around them. Over time, this approach allows them to refine their awareness, only welcoming entities that align with their highest intentions.

Offering gratitude and reverence strengthens the relationship between the practitioner and the spiritual entities. After each interaction, the seeker expresses gratitude, either through a quiet moment of reflection, a spoken word of thanks, or a symbolic offering such as flowers or incense. This act of appreciation solidifies the bond, showing that the practitioner honors the guidance received. Over time, this mutual respect deepens the connection, creating a sense of companionship between the seeker and the spiritual entities they engage with. This gratitude reinforces the practitioner's commitment to maintaining integrity and humility in all interactions.

For advanced practitioners, channeling messages from spiritual entities can be a powerful tool for receiving guidance. Channeling involves entering a meditative state, allowing thoughts or words from a spiritual entity to flow through them. This practice requires both trust and surrender, as the seeker remains open to receiving messages without judgment or interference. Channeling may be experienced as a stream of words, images, or feelings that convey insight or encouragement. The practitioner records these messages in a journal for reflection, observing how the guidance aligns with their inner journey and life circumstances.

Dream encounters with spiritual entities offer another dimension to this connection. The seeker sets an intention before sleep, asking for guidance or insight from a particular entity. Often, these entities appear in dreams as familiar or symbolic figures, delivering messages that bypass the conscious mind. Upon waking, the practitioner reflects on these encounters, paying close attention to any emotions, symbols, or messages that arise. Dream encounters become a sacred meeting ground where the boundaries of consciousness dissolve, and the practitioner receives wisdom that flows seamlessly into their waking life.

Consecrating personal items as channels for connection strengthens the practitioner's ability to attune to specific entities. An object—such as a stone, a piece of jewelry, or a candle—can be consecrated through intention, holding it in a state of meditation and asking for it to serve as a conduit to the chosen entity. This item becomes a focal point for the practitioner, helping them feel connected even outside formal practices. When they hold or wear this object, they are reminded of the guidance and support offered by the spiritual entity, carrying that presence with them into all aspects of life.

The practice of invoking protection is especially important as the practitioner navigates deeper realms of spiritual connection. They may visualize a sphere of protective light around themselves, calling upon a trusted guardian entity to shield them from unhelpful energies. The practitioner can also use protective symbols, such as sacred geometry or traditional Gnostic signs, in their space to reinforce the boundary between their personal energy and the spiritual world. This practice establishes a foundation of safety, ensuring that all connections made are aligned with their well-being.

At this stage, understanding the messages and archetypes that emerge becomes central to the practitioner's journey. Spiritual entities often communicate in symbolic language, with archetypal figures such as the healer, the warrior, or the guide appearing to embody qualities the practitioner needs to integrate. By interpreting these archetypal presences, the seeker gains insight into aspects of themselves, understanding how each entity reflects elements of their own psyche and spiritual path. These encounters encourage self-reflection, helping the practitioner embrace and integrate each quality represented by the archetypes they encounter.

An advanced Gnostic practice is the invocation of angelic or higher-dimensional entities for guidance and illumination. Angelic presences are revered for their high vibration and alignment with divine wisdom. The seeker may call upon these entities in moments of need, visualizing their energy as a pure, radiant light that brings peace and clarity. This invocation is often accompanied by a mantra, prayer, or silent reverence, inviting the angelic presence to provide insight or healing. The practitioner feels an elevated state of awareness in these moments, understanding that this connection transcends the personal and touches the universal.

In their interactions with spiritual entities, the seeker also learns the importance of integration, taking time to absorb and reflect upon the insights received. After an interaction, they may feel a shift in perception, a renewed sense of purpose, or clarity regarding a specific aspect of their life. Integration involves meditation, journaling, or simple moments of contemplation, allowing the messages from the entity to settle and resonate. The seeker recognizes that these connections are not mere experiences but seeds of transformation that, when integrated, become part of their ongoing spiritual evolution.

As the practitioner matures in these practices, they may develop a personal system of invocation and connection unique to their journey. This personal approach evolves as the practitioner understands which symbols, words, and practices resonate most deeply with their spirit. By personalizing their rituals, the seeker creates a powerful framework that strengthens their connection with spiritual entities, honoring the individuality of their path while staying true to the universal principles of gnosis.

In these advanced practices, the Gnostic seeker experiences a profound shift, where spiritual entities are no longer external presences but reflections of the divine qualities within. Each encounter is a step toward gnosis, guiding the practitioner to deeper self-knowledge and a greater understanding of the interconnectedness of all beings. Through this ongoing relationship, the seeker experiences a unity with the spiritual realm that extends beyond individual identity, connecting them to the boundless mysteries of the divine.

This chapter on advanced connection with spiritual entities reaffirms the path of reverence, discernment, and humility. Each practice serves to deepen the practitioner's awareness and expand their inner world, allowing them to walk hand-in-hand with spiritual allies on the journey to self-realization. As these bonds deepen, the seeker becomes a bridge between worlds, embodying wisdom that touches both the earthly and the divine, illuminating their path with the guiding light of the spiritual entities that accompany them.

Chapter 19
Inner Silence Practices

In the path of Gnosticism, silence is not simply an absence of sound but a potent state of inner quiet where the soul can connect directly with the divine. This practice of cultivating inner silence opens a pathway to the deeper self, allowing thoughts, emotions, and distractions to settle. For the Gnostic seeker, achieving inner silence is essential, providing a sanctuary for inner exploration and spiritual clarity.

The journey into silence begins with understanding the power of a quieted mind, where the continual chatter of thoughts is gently subdued, creating space for insight to arise. This quieting process begins with attention to breath. The practitioner takes slow, deliberate breaths, feeling each inhale and exhale as a gentle rhythm that pulls awareness inward. With each breath, they imagine a stillness washing over their mind, releasing tension and allowing thoughts to fade into the background. This conscious breathing slows the mind, offering the first glimpse of the quiet presence beneath the noise.

Mindful observation is another foundational practice for achieving inner silence, where the practitioner becomes aware of thoughts without engaging or resisting them. In a comfortable seated position, they observe each thought that arises, letting it come and go without judgment. This approach teaches them that thoughts are transient, like clouds passing across the sky, and do not require action. As this habit of non-attachment grows, the seeker finds a deep, stable silence behind the passing thoughts, a still point that exists independent of mental activity.

With the mind beginning to quiet, the practitioner then uses focused visualization techniques to deepen the silence further. A common visualization involves picturing a serene landscape—perhaps a quiet forest, a still lake, or an endless sky—where there is no disturbance. The practitioner places themselves in this peaceful setting, feeling its calmness infuse their consciousness. In this visualized space, they experience a suspension of external noise and inner dialogue, immersed fully in the quietude. This visualization becomes a powerful tool, a refuge that the seeker can revisit each time they sit in meditation.

To sustain inner silence, the Gnostic practitioner learns to refine their sensitivity to subtle energies. In silence, energies once too subtle to perceive begin to reveal themselves. The practitioner may feel a gentle warmth or tingling within, a quiet but unmistakable energy that represents the inner life force. By turning their attention to this energy, they shift focus from thoughts to a state of presence that lies beyond mental activity. The practitioner becomes more attuned to this silent vitality, realizing it as a steady, unchanging aspect of the self.

Intentional pauses are also practiced during daily life to extend the presence of silence beyond meditation. The seeker pauses for a few seconds at different moments—whether during conversation, activity, or a simple walk. In each pause, they redirect awareness inward, feeling the stillness within. These brief moments create space, breaking the habitual flow of thought and action, reminding the practitioner of their inner sanctuary. Over time, these pauses lengthen and deepen, allowing the silence to be carried effortlessly throughout the day.

Another technique used to access inner silence is the silent mantra. Unlike vocal mantras, which resonate externally, the silent mantra is repeated only in the mind, creating a quiet vibration that draws awareness inward. The practitioner selects a word or short phrase that resonates deeply with them, one that embodies qualities such as peace, unity, or divinity. With each repetition, the mantra's meaning fills their awareness, overshadowing distracting thoughts. This silent mantra becomes a comforting rhythm that leads the seeker further into stillness.

As the Gnostic practitioner continues these practices, they may experience moments of mental fasting, where they consciously refrain from mental activity altogether. This does not imply the complete absence of thought but rather a state where thoughts arise less frequently, and when they do, they are gentle and non-intrusive. In this state, the practitioner feels a lightness, as if freed from the usual weight of mental engagement. This mental fasting rejuvenates the mind, enabling it to function more clearly and peacefully.

With regular practice, the seeker finds that inner silence is not merely a state to be reached but a space that exists perpetually within. Listening in silence then becomes a spiritual practice, where the practitioner remains in this silent awareness, open to any insights, messages, or intuitions that arise from the depths. This silence is not an empty void but a receptive space filled with subtle understanding. The practitioner learns to trust this quiet wisdom, realizing that true knowledge often emerges in moments of stillness, rather than in active searching.

Embracing emptiness forms the culmination of the initial inner silence practice. Here, the practitioner surrenders fully to silence, allowing it to envelop every part of their being. In this surrender, they experience a profound peace, a realization that beyond the mind's activity lies an essence untouched by thought or form. This state of emptiness brings a sense of unity, where the seeker feels interconnected with the whole of existence. It is here, in this sacred silence, that the divine is most intimately encountered, as a presence within and beyond the self.

The Gnostic path regards this inner silence as a sacred foundation, a space where the divine speaks not through words but through the presence of peace, understanding, and unity. Through these practices, the seeker opens to a state of awareness that transcends the personal, experiencing silence as a vast, unbounded space within their own soul.

As the Gnostic practitioner advances in the art of inner silence, they enter a deeper realm where silence transforms from a temporary state into a profound experience of union with the inner self. This expanded practice is a journey into a silence that penetrates the spirit, revealing insights and bringing the seeker to the threshold of the divine.

The first step in deepening inner silence is mental fasting, where the practitioner engages in prolonged periods of quietude, consciously refraining from active thought. Through this practice, thoughts naturally slow, and the mind experiences a spacious calm. To prepare, the seeker dedicates intentional time—perhaps a day or a series of hours—when they will engage in minimal external activity and focus on inward awareness. During these periods, the practitioner observes each thought as it arises, then gently releases it, allowing the mind to settle into a natural state of rest. This intentional fasting from thought cultivates a profound inner peace, reducing mental noise and bringing clarity.

Building on this is the practice of advanced concentration techniques, where the practitioner sustains silence by focusing intensely on a single point of awareness. Whether focusing on the breath, a candle flame, or a simple object, this practice strengthens the seeker's ability to maintain uninterrupted silence. Concentration narrows the attention, keeping distractions at bay and allowing the mind to deepen into stillness. As the practitioner's concentration strengthens, they may experience a profound quiet that feels almost tangible, a silence that permeates both mind and body.

Sound fasting is a powerful practice in this advanced stage, where the practitioner refrains from exposure to external sounds, such as speech, music, and electronic noise, for a designated period. This practice, often referred to as silence retreats or sound fasts, creates an environment that mirrors inner stillness. By abstaining from external noise, the practitioner heightens their sensitivity to inner silence, noticing subtle energies and shifts within. This silence serves as an incubator, where layers of inner chatter dissolve, revealing insights from the depths of the spirit.

In addition to external silence, the Gnostic practitioner learns the art of emotional stillness, a quieting of the heart's reactive tendencies. Emotional stillness involves observing emotions as they arise, whether anger, joy, or sadness, without attaching to or resisting them. By simply witnessing each emotion with acceptance, the practitioner creates space around it, allowing it to fade naturally. This emotional silence leads to inner harmony, where the heart remains unshaken by external events, fostering a resilient and centered state of being.

At this stage, the seeker may also explore silent communion, a practice of silent prayer or communion with the divine without words or thoughts. This communion is an expression of the soul's reverence, a moment of intimate connection where the seeker feels enveloped in divine presence. In silent communion, there is no need for words or formal prayer; instead, the practitioner rests in an open state, welcoming whatever arises from the connection. Through silent communion, the practitioner experiences a profound sense of unity, as if the silence itself carries the presence of the divine.

The art of sacred waiting deepens the journey of inner silence further. In this practice, the practitioner sits in silence without any expectation, simply waiting for insight, guidance, or inner peace to arise naturally. Sacred waiting is an active form of patience, where the seeker allows understanding to unfold without forcing it. In this waiting, moments of pure awareness arise, and the practitioner often feels a sense of spaciousness or timelessness. Insights that emerge in these moments carry a clarity and wisdom that words often fail to express.

As the seeker becomes more attuned to silence, they may experience the silent witness, a state in which they become the observer of both inner and outer phenomena without identification. In this state, the practitioner feels separate from thoughts, emotions, and sensory experiences, watching them come and go as an impartial observer. The silent witness brings a profound sense of freedom, as the practitioner realizes they are not their thoughts or emotions but rather the awareness in which all these arise and pass. This witnessing silence is a key aspect of gnosis, a deep recognition of the eternal self beyond the mind.

With practice, the seeker moves into non-dual awareness, a state of unity where the boundaries between self and other dissolve, and all of existence is experienced as interconnected. In this state, silence becomes an expression of oneness, where there is no separation between the observer and the observed. The seeker feels a deep, expansive awareness, free from any sense of individual identity. This non-dual awareness is an experience of profound peace, where silence itself becomes a teacher, revealing the interconnectedness of all things.

Another advanced practice is meditating on the void, where the seeker explores the concept of emptiness or "the void" in Gnostic tradition. The void is not a barren emptiness but a space brimming with potential, a state where all forms arise and dissolve. The practitioner focuses on this concept, embracing the absence of form, thought, or identity, realizing that beneath all creation lies an eternal, silent source. Meditating on the void brings the practitioner into contact with the infinite, a state where silence holds the mysteries of existence itself.

The practice of silent ecstasy is often experienced at this level, a state of profound joy and contentment that arises in deep silence. In silent ecstasy, there is no thought, emotion, or desire— only an overwhelming sense of bliss and union with the divine. The practitioner feels as though they are one with the silence itself, experiencing a joy that is pure, unconditioned, and eternal. This silent ecstasy is a gift of deep inner work, an experience that reminds the seeker of the beauty and mystery that silence holds.

In these advanced stages, the practitioner recognizes that silence is no longer merely an internal experience but a quality that radiates outward, affecting the world around them. Carrying silence into action becomes a natural extension of the practice, where the seeker learns to engage in daily tasks while maintaining an inner state of peace. Whether in conversation, work, or routine activities, the practitioner holds onto a core of silence, allowing them to act with greater awareness, compassion, and presence. In this way, silence becomes a living practice, present in every moment.

This chapter on advanced inner silence practices leads the Gnostic practitioner into the mysteries of existence, showing that silence is a doorway to the divine within and beyond. Each practice serves as a guide, inviting the seeker to explore the depths of consciousness where words, thoughts, and even the self dissolve into pure awareness. Through these experiences, the practitioner realizes that silence is not an absence but the fullest presence, a state where the divine speaks in whispers of peace, unity, and eternal truth. In this silence, the Gnostic seeker finds a sanctuary of wisdom, a space that is timeless, boundless, and eternally connected to the divine.

Chapter 20
Liberation Ritual

In the Gnostic path, liberation is both the goal and the journey—an inner release from the bindings of thought, emotion, and identity that obscure the soul's true nature. This chapter begins with a foundational practice: the liberation ritual. The ritual serves as a rite of passage, a powerful tool for freeing oneself from internal attachments, emotional chains, and deep-seated fears that prevent spiritual growth. Here, liberation is seen not merely as freedom from external circumstances, but as a profound internal release, a shedding of layers that reveal the divine spark within.

To prepare for this ritual, the practitioner begins by setting an intention for liberation, a clear, heartfelt statement of their desire to transcend whatever inner blocks they seek to release. This intention creates a mental and spiritual focus that aligns the mind, body, and spirit. It is in this focused state that the practitioner can confront and release the hidden obstacles that dwell in the subconscious. The intention, whether spoken aloud or written down, becomes the first act of liberation, a declaration that the practitioner is ready to leave behind old patterns and embrace the light within.

The ritual space is then prepared, and it is essential to create a setting that reflects the inner sanctity of this moment. The practitioner may choose a private, quiet location, adorned with elements that symbolize purity and release, such as a white candle, fresh water, or incense. Each element represents aspects of liberation: the candle for clarity, water for purification, and incense for the spirit's ascent. Creating this sacred space allows the seeker to step into a realm where physical surroundings mirror the inner act of release, setting the stage for deep transformation.

The ritual itself often begins with guided breathwork, a tool for anchoring the mind and calming the emotions. The practitioner takes slow, deliberate breaths, envisioning each inhalation as drawing in light, while each exhalation releases tension, worry, and attachment. With each breath, they imagine themselves loosening the mental and emotional chains that bind them, creating space for freedom. This breathing pattern becomes a rhythm, a meditative state that paves the way for the deeper stages of the ritual.

Visualization is central to the liberation ritual, where the practitioner pictures themselves as wrapped in layers or chains representing fears, desires, past experiences, or roles they have outgrown. With each exhale, they visualize these bindings dissolving, breaking away to reveal an inner radiance. They may see these as knots that unravel or as heavy layers that fall away, leaving them feeling lighter, freer. This visualization allows the practitioner to confront and release attachments in a tangible way, seeing and feeling the liberation within their body and mind.

The next stage of the ritual involves affirmations of release, spoken aloud or silently, as the seeker acknowledges and lets go of each burden. These affirmations may be as simple as, "I release all that no longer serves my growth," or as specific as naming a particular fear or resentment. Each affirmation is a vow of freedom, an act of power that reinforces the seeker's commitment to liberation. Spoken with conviction, these words break the subconscious ties that hold these attachments in place, allowing the seeker to let them go fully.

A symbolic gesture of release follows, often involving a physical representation of what the seeker wishes to release. This may take the form of a small object or a written list of past attachments, fears, or doubts. In the sacred space, the practitioner ceremonially releases this symbol—perhaps by burning it, burying it, or casting it into water. This act serves as a final release, a physical demonstration of the inner commitment to freedom. As the object transforms or disappears, the practitioner experiences a sense of finality, a symbolic closing of the past to make way for new growth.

After the symbolic release, meditative reflection ensues. The practitioner sits in silence, feeling the new lightness within. Here, they open themselves to any insights, sensations, or guidance that arise from the act of liberation. This reflection allows the energy of release to settle, filling the space once occupied by attachments with calmness and clarity. It is in this quietude that the seeker may sense a profound inner stillness, a momentary union with the true self, unburdened by past limitations.

To seal the ritual, a closing affirmation of gratitude and freedom is spoken. The practitioner acknowledges the journey, giving thanks for the strength to let go and for the new freedom they now embody. This affirmation reinforces their commitment to maintain this state of liberation, consciously choosing thoughts, emotions, and actions that align with their newfound freedom. In this closing moment, the seeker feels an internal shift, a subtle but powerful change that marks a new beginning on their spiritual path.

This liberation ritual also emphasizes the need for grounding as the final step. After such an intense release, the practitioner grounds themselves by feeling the physical connection to their surroundings, to the earth, and to their body. This grounding may involve touching the ground, drinking water, or a few deep breaths to reconnect with the here and now. By grounding, the seeker integrates the experience into their daily life, bringing the energy of liberation from the ritual into their every step.

Through this ritual, the Gnostic practitioner does not simply let go of old burdens—they transform their inner landscape, clearing the way for deeper spiritual experiences. Each time this ritual is performed, another layer of attachment dissolves, revealing more of the soul's true essence. In this practice of liberation, the seeker learns that freedom is not a distant goal but a lived reality, available with every conscious choice to release what no longer serves the path.

In the days following the ritual, the practitioner may feel a profound sense of renewal, a feeling of weightlessness, and an openness to life. They may experience insights, dreams, or a heightened sensitivity to their own thoughts and emotions. This post-ritual period is an essential time for reflection and self-awareness, as the new space created within is ripe for growth and the birth of new intentions.

The liberation ritual is a powerful gateway to spiritual autonomy, marking the soul's ongoing journey toward enlightenment. In this practice, the Gnostic seeker comes to understand that liberation is a path of continual release and renewal, a process of shedding the unnecessary to embrace the essential. Each time they engage in this ritual, they step closer to the divine, liberated from the confines of the past and free to walk the path of true spiritual awakening.

As the Gnostic practitioner delves deeper into the liberation ritual, they begin to discover its power not only as a tool for personal release but as a pathway toward direct spiritual transformation. While the first phase introduces fundamental techniques for releasing attachments, this expanded ritual guides the seeker through more profound practices that enhance the effects, bringing an experience of unity and profound peace.

In this deeper phase, the practitioner begins with an extended period of contemplation, setting the stage by silently revisiting the intentions from the initial liberation ritual. They clarify and strengthen these intentions, reaching further into any attachments, fears, or emotions they wish to transcend. This reflection is a powerful preparatory act, inviting the seeker to embrace all aspects of their inner world—shadow and light—with acceptance. The acknowledgment of hidden emotions, unmet desires, or patterns provides a foundation for an even more profound release.

To deepen the practice, the practitioner incorporates mantras of liberation, drawn from the Gnostic tradition or chosen for their resonance with freedom and spiritual release. These mantras, repeated silently or aloud, function as vibrations that gradually dissolve inner resistances and invite a shift in consciousness. By focusing intently on the mantra, the practitioner aligns their inner and outer energies, centering themselves in a state receptive to profound transformation. In this phase, each sound, each syllable, becomes a vehicle for release, carrying away lingering attachments and embedding freedom within the soul.

At the heart of this advanced liberation ritual is the invocation of guiding energies or archetypes, calling upon symbols of strength, wisdom, and transformation from the Gnostic tradition. The practitioner might invoke the presence of Sophia, the Gnostic embodiment of divine wisdom, or another archetype that represents the guidance needed on their path. This invitation creates a sacred connection, a sense of support that empowers the seeker to move through deep emotional and spiritual layers with courage. Through this invocation, the practitioner understands that they are not alone in their quest, that spiritual forces accompany and support them.

To amplify the transformative power of the ritual, the practitioner integrates visualization techniques that anchor the liberation experience within the physical body. They might visualize light flowing into each part of the body, cleansing and illuminating, dissolving any blockages that remain. This visualization allows the seeker to experience liberation not as an abstract concept but as a tangible, physical sensation. As the body feels lighter, freer, and infused with a radiant energy, the soul naturally aligns with this state of openness, experiencing liberation on all levels.

The ritual also incorporates the use of sacred symbols as tools for grounding the energy of liberation. A particular symbol—be it a crystal, an ankh, or a spiral—is chosen to represent the seeker's release. As they meditate on this symbol, they imbue it with the essence of liberation, and it becomes a talisman that carries the energy of freedom beyond the ritual space. Each time the practitioner sees or touches this symbol, it serves as a reminder of their commitment to remain unattached and in tune with their true self.

To conclude this extended ritual, the seeker performs a final act of integration, a meditation that harmonizes the newly liberated self with the energy of the divine. In this quiet space, the practitioner invites the divine light to fill the new space created within. They sit in stillness, open to any insights, messages, or sensations that arise. In this silence, the energy of the ritual settles deeply within, creating a sense of unity and wholeness that feels both grounding and expansive. This integration is essential; it allows the practitioner to retain the experience of liberation as an enduring presence in daily life.

As the ritual concludes, a closing affirmation of divine union is spoken, expressing gratitude for the transformation and the newfound freedom. This affirmation is simple yet powerful, capturing the essence of the ritual in words. By affirming their connection with the divine and their liberation from inner constraints, the practitioner seals the experience, carrying forward its energy into every thought, action, and interaction that follows.

In the days and weeks after the ritual, the practitioner may experience shifts—clarity, emotional release, or even vivid dreams. This post-ritual phase is seen as a period of spiritual "rebirth," where the inner landscape is rearranged, allowing new insights, perspectives, and understandings to emerge.

Chapter 21
Kundalini Energy

The exploration of Kundalini energy in Gnosticism introduces the practitioner to one of the most profound sources of inner transformation—a dormant, yet vibrant spiritual force said to reside at the base of the spine. Awakening Kundalini is considered an advanced and sacred process, often depicted as the rising of a coiled serpent, symbolizing the latent spiritual potential within every individual. In Gnosticism, Kundalini is viewed not only as an energy for personal growth but as a key to transcendent insight and divine unity.

The practitioner begins by preparing mind and body to awaken this energy gradually, understanding that Kundalini's full force cannot be unlocked at once without potentially overwhelming effects. The initial steps involve grounding and centering practices designed to stabilize the physical and energetic bodies, creating a solid foundation for safely working with this potent force. These preparatory practices are essential, as they establish a safe space for the seeker to connect with this energy in a controlled and harmonious way.

Breathing techniques are fundamental in Kundalini activation, acting as the primary tool for stirring the energy gently. The practitioner engages in controlled breath exercises, such as diaphragmatic breathing, where each breath is drawn deep into the belly, filling the lungs fully, then released slowly and steadily. This breathing process is repeated rhythmically, with the intention of loosening any blockages along the spine. With each breath, the seeker visualizes energy moving upward from the base of the spine, slowly paving the way for Kundalini's ascension.

The next stage involves visualization and intention. The practitioner begins by visualizing the Kundalini energy as a coiled serpent at the base of the spine, resting in a state of potentiality. With each breath, they envision this serpent awakening and uncoiling, preparing to rise. This imagery, combined with focused intention, encourages a gentle stirring of the energy. The practitioner sets the intention for this process, asking that the energy rise only as far as their system can safely integrate. This conscious approach is essential in the early stages, as it allows the body and mind to adjust gradually to this new flow of energy.

Body awareness exercises also play a crucial role, encouraging the practitioner to attune to sensations within the body. They focus their awareness on each chakra, or energy center, from the base of the spine to the crown of the head. Beginning with the root chakra, they spend time sensing any warmth, tingling, or other sensations, gradually moving upward to explore the entire pathway along which Kundalini energy will eventually flow. By engaging in this mindful exploration, the seeker establishes a deep connection with their inner energy system, preparing it for the eventual ascension of Kundalini.

Physical postures, particularly those associated with grounding and spine alignment, are also integral in the early stages of Kundalini work. Simple postures, such as sitting cross-legged with the spine straight, help open and align the energy channels along the spine. With each posture, the practitioner focuses on relaxing the body and releasing tension, ensuring that the energy pathway is as open and receptive as possible. This physical alignment is mirrored by an inner alignment, as the practitioner consciously releases mental and emotional blocks that could impede the flow of Kundalini energy.

In this initial stage, guided meditation is used to gently engage with Kundalini energy. The practitioner is guided to focus awareness at the base of the spine, visualizing a warm, glowing light that represents the energy of Kundalini. With each breath, this light grows a bit brighter, a bit warmer, but remains calm and steady. This visualization strengthens the mind-body connection and allows the practitioner to gradually attune to Kundalini's presence without forcing it to rise prematurely. By simply focusing on this light, the seeker begins to feel the energy's quiet strength, a latent power waiting to awaken fully.

Chanting and sound vibrations are also introduced as methods to stimulate and harmonize Kundalini energy. Certain sounds and mantras, particularly those resonating with the lower chakras, are chanted to awaken and direct this energy upwards. Each sound is intoned slowly, with intention, allowing its vibration to reach and awaken deeper levels of consciousness. The seeker uses each chant to focus on specific energy centers, drawing the Kundalini energy upward in a calm and balanced way. This chanting not only activates Kundalini energy but also establishes a protective vibration around the practitioner, fostering a sense of safety and grounding.

Throughout this practice, the seeker remains conscious of physical sensations and emotional responses, which may include warmth, tingling, or even unexpected emotions surfacing as blockages dissolve. It's common for practitioners to feel a variety of emotions as Kundalini begins to stir—old memories, hidden fears, or unresolved experiences may arise. The seeker is encouraged to observe these experiences without judgment, recognizing them as signs of inner cleansing and energy movement. Each sensation or emotion is met with acceptance, acknowledged as part of the process of awakening this transformative force.

One of the most valuable aspects of this phase is journaling and self-reflection, where the practitioner records their sensations, insights, and any symbolic images or emotions that arise. This reflective process allows the seeker to track their progress and notice subtle changes within themselves as Kundalini awakens. Journaling serves as a bridge between the conscious and subconscious mind, helping the practitioner to integrate experiences and deepen their understanding of Kundalini's effect on their spiritual path.

As the chapter closes, the practitioner is reminded of the importance of patience and self-care. Kundalini is a lifelong journey, one that unfolds in stages, each more transformative than the last. The practitioner is encouraged to proceed gradually, respecting their body's natural rhythm and ensuring that they integrate each new level of energy before moving forward. Self-care practices, such as adequate rest, grounding exercises, and nourishing food, are emphasized to support the body as it adjusts to the increased energy.

The first stage of Kundalini awakening is a gentle introduction to an immense spiritual potential, one that can open doors to higher consciousness and profound inner wisdom. In this journey, the practitioner learns that Kundalini is more than just energy; it is a path of transformation, an invitation to transcend ordinary awareness and discover the boundless depths of the soul. With patience, dedication, and reverence, the Gnostic seeker steps onto a sacred path, one where Kundalini's rising light gradually illuminates the divine essence within.

As the seeker advances in their work with Kundalini energy, they are now prepared to explore deeper practices that support a safe, mindful, and transformative rise of this powerful force. In Gnosticism, Kundalini is not merely energy but a living symbol of spiritual ascent, a gradual journey of awareness that unites body, mind, and spirit. The initial steps have prepared the seeker's energy system, making way for the next phase, where focused techniques guide the Kundalini upward along the spine, through each chakra, opening pathways to heightened consciousness and mystical insight.

At the heart of this practice is advanced breathwork, where the seeker learns to direct Kundalini energy with greater precision. The breath, now more than a calming tool, becomes the means to channel energy upward, moving it mindfully through the chakras. The seeker practices a breath known as Kundalini pranayama, a rhythmic technique where inhalations pull energy up through the spine while exhalations ground it gently back down. This controlled breathing allows the practitioner to sense and guide the energy, gradually awakening it further with each session. They visualize the breath as a carrier of light, connecting with Kundalini and guiding it upwards, inch by inch, chakra by chakra.

In addition to pranayama, focused visualization plays a pivotal role. The practitioner visualizes the energy as a radiant light or a gentle flame traveling upward, pausing at each chakra along the way. At the root, the light pulses with stability; at the sacral, it becomes warmer and more vibrant; at the solar plexus, it shines with strength. As the light ascends, it interacts with the qualities of each chakra, expanding the seeker's awareness of their emotional, mental, and spiritual states. By visualizing Kundalini's movement, the practitioner nurtures a balanced and deliberate rise, ensuring that each energy center is prepared and aligned.

In this stage, sound resonance takes on a heightened role. The practitioner uses vocal toning or mantra chanting not only to activate but to sustain the Kundalini flow. Specific sounds, such as the seed mantras for each chakra, are chanted slowly, allowing their vibrations to resonate deeply within each energy center. For example, the sound LAM resonates with the root chakra, grounding the energy, while VAM activates the sacral, encouraging emotional release and vitality. Each chant serves as a bridge, guiding the energy upwards in harmony with the qualities of the respective chakras. This practice refines the Kundalini flow, clearing any residual blocks and allowing the energy to ascend naturally.

As Kundalini reaches the heart chakra, the practitioner engages in heart-centered meditation, a phase of deep compassion and connection. Here, the focus is on embracing the openness and unconditional love that arises as the heart center awakens. The practitioner meditates on a feeling of warmth and expansion, visualizing the energy as a soft, radiant light. This light represents both the personal heart and the universal heart, merging individual and cosmic consciousness. This meditation allows Kundalini to pass through the heart with ease, softening the practitioner's inner landscape and nurturing a sense of oneness.

From the heart, Kundalini flows to the throat chakra, where expressive exercises encourage the seeker to release the energy through sound or movement. This chakra is the gateway to authentic expression, and the practitioner may feel an urge to voice insights, chant, or even move in rhythm with the energy. This release enables the practitioner to express deeper truths and resonate with inner clarity. Here, the energy refines, shifting from emotional release to spiritual resonance, allowing the seeker to speak, sing, or write from a place of divine inspiration.

At the third eye, or the ajna chakra, the seeker engages in a practice of heightened perception. In this center, Kundalini energy unlocks intuitive vision, and the practitioner practices deep meditation, focusing on this chakra to cultivate insight and clarity. They visualize a glowing light between the eyebrows, feeling a gentle pressure as Kundalini energy activates their intuitive faculties. In this heightened state, visions, insights, or symbolic imagery may arise, offering the practitioner a glimpse into the subtle realms of consciousness. This practice enhances the seeker's intuitive sensitivity, opening pathways to wisdom beyond rational understanding.

Finally, the practitioner guides Kundalini energy to the crown chakra, sahasrara, the center of spiritual unity. Here, they experience the energy as a sensation of boundlessness, a sense of expansion that dissolves the boundaries of individual identity. They sit in silence, allowing the energy to radiate from the top of the head, merging with the divine source, experiencing union with all that is. In this space of oneness, Kundalini energy completes its ascent, bringing the practitioner to a state of transcendent awareness. This experience, often brief yet profound, offers a direct encounter with the Gnostic concept of Pleroma—the fullness of divine reality.

After the ascent, grounding and integration practices are essential, as the practitioner needs to bring the energy back into balance within their daily life. Grounding exercises, such as deep breathing, mindful walking, or even tactile connection with the earth, help to anchor the heightened awareness. This grounding consolidates the experience, enabling the practitioner to integrate insights into practical wisdom, making Kundalini not just an experience but a guiding force in daily life.

The post-ritual phase also encourages introspective journaling, as the practitioner reflects on the sensations, visions, or emotions that arose during the ascent. Writing these experiences fosters a deeper understanding of the Kundalini process, allowing insights to crystallize and revealing personal patterns or truths that the energy uncovered. This practice becomes a valuable tool, documenting the practitioner's evolution as they continue to work with Kundalini.

To close this chapter, the practitioner is reminded that the Kundalini journey is one of ongoing commitment, patience, and reverence. They are encouraged to approach this energy as a sacred ally on the path to divine union. With each session, they grow in strength, wisdom, and insight, moving closer to the soul's true nature. Each rise of Kundalini energy is unique, illuminating new aspects of consciousness and transforming the seeker in subtle, yet profound, ways.

This phase of the Kundalini path emphasizes balance—awakening without haste, allowing each chakra to harmonize, and respecting the body's rhythms. Through this journey, the Gnostic practitioner gains insight into the spiritual alchemy of Kundalini, understanding that it is not merely an experience but a lifelong unfolding of the soul's potential. In this sacred ascent, they come to realize that Kundalini energy is an inner teacher, guiding them step-by-step toward unity with the divine, each ascent a return to the Pleroma, the divine fullness that resides within.

Chapter 22
The Art of Detachment

In the Gnostic path, detachment is an alchemical process that frees the soul from entanglements that obscure its light. It involves loosening the grip of external influences, emotional ties, and material possessions that bind one to the transient realm, inhibiting the soul's ascent toward higher consciousness. For Gnostics, this process is not about withdrawal from life but about finding a balance that enables spiritual freedom and genuine presence. Detachment, when practiced mindfully, purifies one's intentions and draws the practitioner closer to an inner stillness where the true self resides.

The journey of detachment begins with a reflection on personal attachments. The practitioner is encouraged to turn inward and examine areas where dependencies or lingering emotions restrict their inner freedom. This phase of the practice is introspective, helping identify what holds emotional weight in daily life—be it material objects, relationships, habits, or even self-concepts. The awareness that arises from this analysis is often profound, revealing the extent to which the ego clings to identities and objects for validation and security. Gnostic detachment encourages the practitioner to recognize that these attachments are constructs that create barriers to experiencing the Pleroma—the fullness of divine reality.

One initial practice is the ritual of release, where the practitioner consciously acknowledges and symbolically releases attachments. In a private, sacred space, they select a symbolic item representing a particular attachment—something that can embody a lingering need, memory, or even an unfulfilled desire. Holding the item, the practitioner meditates on its significance, noting the emotions or memories it evokes, and then, in a ceremonial act, lets it go. This ritual may involve burying, donating, or simply moving the item to a new location, signifying a release of its psychological hold. This practice acts as a bridge between the mental and the material, transforming intangible attachments into concrete, release-oriented actions.

A fundamental aspect of detachment is learning to find peace within impermanence. Gnostic philosophy views the material world as transient, a realm crafted by the Demiurge, where permanence is an illusion. By confronting this impermanence, practitioners come to terms with the fluid nature of all things, including themselves. In this pursuit, they adopt the practice of meditative reflection on impermanence, where they sit in quiet contemplation, observing their own fleeting thoughts, emotions, and bodily sensations. This practice teaches that clinging to impermanent states causes suffering; by letting go of these attachments, practitioners cultivate a state of serenity and awareness that endures beyond changing conditions.

Another essential practice is the daily mantra of liberation, where the practitioner adopts a simple phrase that encapsulates the essence of detachment, such as, "I release what no longer serves my highest path." Repeating this mantra daily strengthens the mind's alignment with the heart's desire for spiritual freedom. This mantra is not only spoken aloud but held silently in the mind throughout the day, especially when feelings of attachment arise. The mantra helps refocus intentions, reminding the practitioner of their deeper purpose and creating a space within where divine wisdom may arise unimpeded by transient concerns.

Observing relationships is also an integral part of detachment. In relationships, attachments often form through expectations, dependencies, or unfulfilled needs projected onto others. The practitioner is encouraged to mindfully evaluate the dynamics of their relationships, reflecting on whether each one promotes mutual growth and understanding or perpetuates a cycle of dependency. This is not an exercise in judgment, but rather in clarity, inviting the practitioner to approach relationships with open-hearted compassion rather than clinging. This practice fosters healthy boundaries, allowing one to relate to others from a place of respect and kindness, rather than from possessiveness or need.

To deepen the journey, the practitioner may engage in a meditation on the soul's independence. Sitting in a quiet, sacred space, they visualize their soul as a radiant sphere of light, whole and complete, existing beyond all attachments and needs. In this visualization, they experience the feeling of profound wholeness, a state unaltered by external circumstances. This practice serves as a reminder that the soul's essence is already free and complete, and that true connection with others and the world does not require dependency but rather the sharing of one's inner light.

Finally, detachment from material possessions is a practice that brings clarity to one's relationship with the physical world. Practitioners are encouraged to simplify their surroundings, keeping only what is meaningful and conducive to their spiritual journey. This practice is not about rejecting the material world but about choosing consciously what one allows into their space and life. By intentionally reducing physical belongings, the practitioner's environment becomes a reflection of their internal clarity, free from the clutter of unnecessary items. This cultivated simplicity extends to all aspects of life, fostering an environment that nurtures spiritual exploration rather than distracting from it.

In embracing detachment, the Gnostic practitioner gradually cultivates a profound sense of liberation. By releasing external attachments and aligning with the essence within, they experience life with greater presence, unburdened by transient concerns. This process opens the pathway to true freedom, where one lives from the authentic self, embodying a state of awareness that is deeply connected yet free from worldly dependencies. This journey of detachment is not one of isolation but a path to deeper connection with the divine, enabling the soul to move freely, unbound, on its sacred journey.

The art of detachment, once initially embraced, evolves into a practice that reaches into every layer of one's being. Where the first steps revealed attachments and loosened their hold, the next phase transforms detachment into a pathway for profound liberation, refining the soul's capacity to interact with the world without clinging, while expanding inner stillness and resilience. Now, detachment shifts from a mindful release into a harmonious alignment with divine freedom, enabling the practitioner to live fully present, unchained by inner or outer demands.

A central practice in deepening detachment is the exercise of compassionate observation. This exercise is a meditation that encourages practitioners to observe their own emotional responses with kindness and detachment, witnessing each feeling and thought as it arises without judgment or reaction. By sitting quietly, breathing slowly, and watching the movement of emotions and thoughts as if they were passing clouds, one becomes skilled at seeing these experiences as transient and ultimately separate from the true self. This compassionate approach allows practitioners to feel without attachment, to engage with life's experiences without becoming lost in them.

Another key practice is letting go through breath work, a technique that draws on the breath to release internal tensions and energetic attachments. The practitioner begins by sitting comfortably, focusing on deep, even breaths. As they inhale, they imagine drawing in a clear, calm energy; with each exhale, they visualize releasing attachments, fears, and concerns. This breathing rhythm aligns body and mind in a state of open receptivity, creating space for clarity and detachment within. Practicing this form of conscious breathing daily instills a calm awareness that naturally begins to dissolve emotional patterns rooted in attachment.

To deepen detachment, Gnostic tradition also incorporates a ritual of surrender. This ritual is performed in a sacred space, and it serves to remind the practitioner of their spiritual journey's ultimate purpose: unity with the divine. It involves the symbolic act of writing down one's attachments, desires, or persistent thoughts on pieces of paper. Each slip of paper represents something that has tethered the practitioner to material or egoic concerns. In a quiet, reverent moment, each paper is burned, symbolizing a release to the divine and an affirmation of trust in the spiritual process. This ritual of surrender fosters a profound sense of release, making way for divine wisdom to guide the practitioner forward without the burden of excessive personal concerns.

A further aspect of detachment involves meditating on impermanence through nature. Spending time in natural settings—a forest, a stream, or a mountainside—reminds the practitioner of the cycles of change that define existence. In nature, all things are in motion, from the turning of the seasons to the growth and decay of living things. Through this meditation, the practitioner reflects on life's natural rhythm of change and becomes more comfortable with the impermanence of all things, including personal experiences, emotions, and material possessions. By witnessing nature's continuous cycle of creation and dissolution, the practitioner gains perspective on their own attachments and allows the wisdom of impermanence to permeate their consciousness.

Another vital method is the practice of non-reactive awareness in daily interactions. As practitioners navigate social encounters, they focus on maintaining an inner state of calm regardless of external events or responses. This means observing interactions as a witness, noticing how attachments might arise in the form of defensiveness, need for approval, or the urge to control outcomes. By holding a steady awareness, the practitioner learns to engage with others from a place of grounded neutrality, releasing the impulse to cling to opinions or outcomes. This approach does not mean indifference but fosters a sincere presence in relationships, a willingness to connect deeply without becoming bound by expectations or fears.

Devotional detachment is another transformative technique, where the practitioner places their intentions, actions, and experiences in service to the divine. Through a quiet dedication of their daily tasks, prayers, and even their challenges to the higher power, they cultivate an attitude that all outcomes belong to a greater purpose. By continually redirecting focus away from self-centered desires and offering everything to the divine, the practitioner gradually achieves freedom from personal attachment to results. This devotional approach builds a perspective rooted in humility, where each action becomes an offering, thereby removing the ego from the equation and allowing for an unburdened experience of life.

A final exercise is contemplative journaling on identity and essence. The practitioner uses journaling as a method for examining the layers of self that hold attachments. In a quiet, reflective setting, they explore questions such as: "Who am I beyond my possessions, roles, and desires?" "What essence remains if everything I cling to is released?" and "What inner strength or peace do I discover in letting go?" This journaling practice takes them beyond the layers of attachment, guiding them toward a realization of the essence that lies within, untouched by the transient nature of external attachments. This exercise is both liberating and empowering, revealing the resilient, unchanging aspect of the self.

As this chapter of detachment deepens, the practitioner is prepared to live with presence and awareness, embracing the richness of life without possessiveness. They are now less a seeker who must grasp and more a witness who is free to experience life's vastness. This maturity in detachment infuses their journey with joy, lightness, and a greater capacity to love, for true detachment opens the heart rather than closing it. This higher detachment is no longer a rejection but an invitation to exist fully—rooted in divine essence, free from unnecessary burdens, and open to the mysteries that await.

Chapter 23
Consciousness Expansion

In the quest to expand consciousness, one steps into realms where the mind's usual boundaries are tested, even dissolved, in favor of experiences that unveil hidden layers of reality. Gnosticism teaches that our conventional perception is only a fragment, and that by transcending the limits of everyday thought, we enter vast fields of awareness where divine truth is encountered directly. The practice of expanding consciousness begins with exercises that challenge the familiar modes of thought and perception, gradually attuning the practitioner to layers of reality beyond the physical and into the mystical.

A foundational practice in expanding consciousness is concentrative meditation on symbols. In Gnosticism, specific symbols hold deep metaphysical meanings that resonate with the psyche's deeper layers. By focusing on symbols like the serpent, the lotus, or geometric forms representing balance and divinity, practitioners enter into meditative states where the symbol acts as a gateway to higher understanding. This exercise involves choosing a symbol that speaks to one's inner journey, placing it at eye level, and allowing focus to remain solely on its form. Slowly, the practitioner lets the mind quiet, allowing the symbolic image to imprint itself, bypassing conscious interpretation and seeding itself in the deeper mind. As sessions progress, the chosen symbol begins to evoke images, sensations, or insights, each of which reveals facets of the symbol's deeper truth and aligns the practitioner with universal patterns of knowledge.

Expanded breathwork is another essential method for widening consciousness. Breathwork in Gnostic practice goes beyond basic calming techniques; it engages the breath as a tool for altering the state of awareness. The practitioner begins with rhythmic breathing—breathing in to a count of four, holding for two, and exhaling to a count of four, gradually extending these intervals. This breathing style awakens latent energetic pathways in the body, enhancing the flow of prana or life energy. With each session, one finds that this practice induces a heightened sense of clarity and often a state of alert stillness where inner vision expands. Breathwork performed consistently attunes the practitioner to subtle energies within and around them, creating a perceptual shift that fosters experiences of interconnectedness.

Gnosticism also teaches mind-body attunement through sensory withdrawal, also known as Pratyahara in Eastern traditions. In a quiet space, practitioners begin by focusing intently on each sense—first the sounds in their surroundings, then tactile sensations, sights, tastes, and smells—becoming acutely aware of each before gradually withdrawing their focus inward. This sensory withdrawal cultivates inner silence and prepares the practitioner for states of higher perception, as the mind no longer clings to external stimuli. Regular practice allows consciousness to move away from the distractions of the material plane, revealing subtler inner landscapes that are usually hidden by the constant noise of sensory input.

Visualization techniques also play a significant role in consciousness expansion. In the astral doorway exercise, the practitioner visualizes a sacred door within their mind's eye, often with a meaningful symbol or word inscribed upon it, symbolizing a passage to expanded awareness. By mentally approaching this door, one imagines touching it, feeling its texture, and slowly opening it to reveal a path that leads deeper into their consciousness. Practiced consistently, this doorway becomes a mental access point, allowing the practitioner to enter realms beyond typical waking awareness. As the technique develops, this visualization exercise can lead to profound experiences of light, symbols, or guidance, each contributing to a gradual widening of consciousness.

Group meditation offers another unique pathway for expanding consciousness, especially within Gnostic communities. In a shared sacred space, the collective intention of expanding awareness harmonizes participants' energies, creating an amplified field. Sitting in a circle, each person focuses on inner silence and holds an openness to spiritual connection. As energies coalesce, practitioners often experience a heightening of their own awareness, as if carried by the collective intention. Group meditation fosters both individual insight and a sense of interconnectedness, mirroring the Gnostic understanding of unity within the divine fullness or Pleroma. This shared experience can often lead to moments of collective vision, where participants report sensing the same colors, images, or symbolic messages, reinforcing the group's unified field of consciousness.

Lastly, reflection on the eternal now is a contemplative exercise designed to free consciousness from the constraints of linear time. By focusing solely on the present moment—free from thoughts of past or future—the practitioner experiences life as a continuous unfolding rather than a sequence of events. In this heightened awareness, one feels the flow of life itself, recognizing the present moment as the only point of true existence. This exercise requires a focused and open mind, best practiced in a natural setting or a quiet space, where distractions are minimal. As the practitioner becomes comfortable with this state of timeless awareness, they may experience a shift where the boundary between self and world softens, and life reveals itself as an interconnected, continuous flow.

This introductory stage of consciousness expansion lays the groundwork for profound spiritual experiences. Each practice gradually opens the practitioner to levels of perception that reveal new dimensions of being, each attuned to spiritual realities and insights that the ordinary mind cannot grasp. By expanding consciousness, one begins to perceive and participate in the greater harmony of the cosmos, experiencing life from a place of awareness that is grounded, open, and profoundly connected to the spiritual realms.

As consciousness continues to expand, the journey moves deeper into territories where reality is no longer confined by sensory perception, reason, or even individual identity. Gnosticism describes this state as a step closer to the Pleroma—the boundless realm of divine fullness. In this advanced stage, practices evolve from exploratory techniques into precise tools for attaining profound experiences, including astral projection, heightened communion with higher planes, and glimpses of spiritual ecstasy that dissolve the illusion of separateness.

One of the central practices in this phase is the Astral Plane Meditation. This meditation is distinct from previous visualizations as it involves the conscious, directed intention of experiencing realms beyond the physical. The practitioner prepares by entering a deep meditative state, clearing the mind of earthly concerns and allowing thoughts to subside. Through rhythmic breathing and by focusing on a symbol associated with ascent—often a spiral staircase or a radiant star—the practitioner visualizes their subtle body rising, detached from the physical. As the awareness shifts, there is a sensation of lightness, a floating sensation in which one finds themselves within a realm that is distinctly different yet intimately connected to consciousness. In this state, the practitioner may observe vivid imagery, encounter beings, or experience teachings conveyed telepathically. With repeated practice, these excursions into the astral plane allow for meaningful and transformative encounters, each expanding the mind's capacity to comprehend existence beyond the limits of matter.

Accompanying astral practices is Spiritual Ecstasy Meditation, a practice designed to align the individual with the divine energies that flow continuously within the universe. This meditation begins with intense breathwork that seeks to quicken the practitioner's vibrational state, using a cadence that gradually accelerates before releasing into silence. In this state, consciousness aligns itself with what Gnosticism refers to as the "light within," where the practitioner experiences a luminous sense of self that is pure awareness, untouched by thought or form. This practice, performed with increasing skill and openness, invites the practitioner into an ecstatic state, a feeling of oneness with the entire universe, where boundaries between the self and the divine dissolve. The sensation is one of boundless energy, love, and profound knowing, where the practitioner understands on an experiential level what cannot be comprehended intellectually. The ecstasy within this state acts as a direct connection to the divine, providing both insight and rejuvenation that influence the practitioner's life profoundly.

Another transformative approach to expanded consciousness is Gnostic Trance Work. In this practice, the practitioner enters a trance through repetitive chanting or intonation of a sacred word, such as "Aeon" or "Sophia." The sound is chosen based on its vibration, which resonates with certain higher frequencies and archetypal energies in the Gnostic tradition. Chanting is done in a low, continuous rhythm, gradually slowing the mind and entrancing the practitioner. As the chant continues, consciousness enters a liminal space where visions, memories, or symbolic messages arise spontaneously, often bringing insight into current spiritual or personal questions. In this state, the conscious mind becomes an observer as hidden wisdom surfaces, providing guidance and revealing truths in response to the practitioner's spiritual needs. As visions unfold, they often feel mythic and deeply personal, illuminating the connection between the individual and universal consciousness.

A practice closely related to trance work is Symbolic Journeying. In Gnosticism, journeying involves mentally traveling into sacred symbols, each serving as an entrance to different layers of consciousness. The practitioner first chooses a potent symbol such as the labyrinth, the tree of life, or an ancient vessel. As they close their eyes and meditate on the image, they begin to mentally "enter" it, following pathways that appear and exploring realms hidden within the symbol itself. Each journey offers revelations unique to the individual, leading them to encounter inner archetypes, guardians, or aspects of divine wisdom. With time, symbolic journeying reveals an inner world rich with wisdom, a tapestry that not only mirrors the practitioner's soul but reflects universal truths embedded within the symbols themselves. This practice encourages direct encounters with the mysteries, making them living, experiential teachings rather than abstract concepts.

Union with the Divine Through Silent Communion represents the culmination of consciousness expansion practices. This is a meditation in which the practitioner reaches for the deepest state of silence, beyond thoughts, beyond even the observer self. Here, the intention is to dissolve all boundaries, entering a profound stillness that reveals the self as inseparable from the divine source. It is an exercise in pure receptivity, where the practitioner neither visualizes nor chants but simply remains open, allowing the sacred presence to emerge. As the silence deepens, the practitioner often perceives an inner radiance, an indescribable presence that seems to permeate everything within and around them. This state is the goal of consciousness expansion in Gnosticism: to experience the self as the divine, to become both the seeker and the sought, the question and the answer, where the universe and the individual merge.

As each technique builds upon the previous, consciousness expands to encompass levels of reality once thought impossible. With dedication and inner clarity, practitioners of these methods glimpse beyond the veil of the ordinary, encountering the divine not as an external force, but as the deepest part of their own being. Through these practices, the Gnostic journey of expanding consciousness becomes a transformative path, leading toward ultimate spiritual freedom and unity with the sacred.

Chapter 24
The Path of the Heart

In Gnosticism, the path of the heart stands as a bridge between intellect and spirit, an essential channel for accessing divine love, compassion, and the true self. To walk this path is to transcend personal barriers and open the deepest layers of the soul to unity with all beings. Gnostic tradition teaches that the heart is the seat of a spiritual intelligence that perceives beyond words and symbols, sensing an interconnectedness that the mind alone cannot fully grasp. Here, compassion emerges not as a virtue to attain but as the natural state of a heart awakened to divine presence.

The practice begins with Opening the Heart Meditation, a quieting exercise to reach the silent depths within. Seated comfortably, the practitioner breathes slowly, each inhalation an invitation to listen more deeply. This is not just a physical breath but a symbolic one, a drawing in of the life force that flows through all creation. As each breath becomes calmer, attention is gently directed to the heart center, visualized as a warm, radiant glow. In time, this inner glow expands, filling the body, then extending outward to encompass the space around the practitioner. Within this space, they may reflect on moments of love and kindness from their own life, allowing the heart center to grow in warmth, creating an inner wellspring of compassion and unity.

As this meditation deepens, practitioners move into Heartful Awareness, an advanced practice for connecting with the divine presence within others. The method is deceptively simple yet profound: in this state, one consciously extends this feeling of warmth and love toward other beings—family, friends, strangers, and even perceived adversaries. With each breath, the practitioner visualizes a light that flows from their heart center to each person they wish to connect with, holding them in thoughts of peace, love, and understanding. In Gnostic thought, the heart serves as the divine lens through which we see and know others as reflections of the divine. As this connection develops, judgment and division begin to dissolve, leaving only a deep awareness of shared divine essence.

Sacred Compassion Exercises further cultivate the heart's boundless capacity for love by focusing on the quality of forgiveness. This phase invites the practitioner to confront emotional barriers that restrict the flow of love, such as resentment, grief, or anger. These emotions, while powerful, are not permanent; they are energies that transform when seen with compassion. The practitioner visualizes holding these emotions within the heart, treating them as sacred parts of their experience, honoring them as lessons. As they accept these parts with kindness rather than rejection, the heart opens wider, expanding the practitioner's ability to see others with the same understanding.

Additionally, Loving-Kindness Chanting is introduced as a method to bring the heart's intentions into the world. The practitioner chants simple phrases in a language of their choice, such as "May all beings be peaceful, may all beings be happy, may all beings be free." Repeating these words rhythmically deepens the resonance of compassion, spreading the heart's energy outward with intention. Gnostics believe that this chanting works as a form of spiritual alchemy, not only aligning the practitioner's inner self with higher states of love but also impacting the collective consciousness. Each uttered phrase becomes a bridge of light between the individual heart and the hearts of all beings.

Another powerful practice in the path of the heart is the Compassionate Breath, which is essential when applying Gnostic principles to daily interactions. The practitioner begins by bringing full attention to the breath, especially in moments of tension or discomfort. As they breathe in, they imagine drawing in understanding, patience, and divine love; as they breathe out, they release all judgments, fears, and personal biases. This practice turns the breath into a source of healing for oneself and others, fostering an immediate sense of peace that makes it possible to respond with empathy rather than reaction. Through compassionate breath, Gnostics learn to embody divine love in every encounter, making each interaction an opportunity for spiritual growth.

Lastly, Inner Devotion through Prayerful Reflection nurtures a deep, continuous bond with the divine. This prayer differs from traditional prayers that ask or seek; it is a silent expression of gratitude and love toward the divine within and around the practitioner. They sit quietly, allowing a sense of reverence and appreciation to rise naturally, offering thanks for the gifts of insight, love, and growth. The heart becomes a vessel for this gratitude, expanding its energy and radiance. In Gnostic tradition, this practice does not seek divine favor but instead cultivates an intimate awareness of divine presence. It is through this reflective devotion that the heart aligns with the divine's unconditional love, experiencing itself as a part of that love.

The path of the heart is a journey of opening, of learning to embrace each layer of experience, feeling, and connection as a sacred expression of life. As practitioners advance on this path, they experience a new dimension of divine reality—one in which love flows effortlessly, unbound by conditions, linking them with others in an unbreakable chain of divine essence. Through these practices, they find that the heart is more than a center of emotion; it is the gateway to the divine, transforming the practitioner's view of themselves, others, and the world.

The path of the heart, once opened, calls for even deeper cultivation. In this stage, practitioners are invited into profound practices of forgiveness, reconciliation, and compassionate transformation, each designed to unlock higher levels of spiritual unity. As this journey unfolds, the heart is trained not only to experience love but to become a vessel through which divine love flows continuously, uniting the self with others and the divine essence.

To deepen this work, Forgiveness Meditation is an essential practice for unburdening the heart. In a seated, quiet posture, the practitioner begins with steady breathing, visualizing the heart as a bright sphere of light. As they breathe, this light grows stronger, illuminating any lingering feelings of resentment, pain, or anger. One by one, the practitioner brings to mind those with whom they share unresolved conflicts, silently acknowledging the pain each situation holds. Rather than rejecting or justifying these emotions, the practitioner invites the energy of forgiveness to transform them. With each breath, they envision releasing the pain into the light, offering forgiveness to the other person and, equally important, to themselves. Over time, this act of forgiveness cleanses the heart, allowing it to return to a state of openness and compassion, no longer held by the weight of past wounds.

Following forgiveness, practitioners enter The Ritual of Reconciliation, a simple yet deeply moving ritual to repair and renew bonds with others, living or deceased. For this ritual, practitioners may set up a small altar space with items representing the person they wish to reconcile with, such as a candle or a small token. In Gnostic understanding, intention has power, and as the practitioner lights the candle, they focus on the light as a symbol of the divine presence within both themselves and the other. Standing or seated before the candle, they speak aloud words of reconciliation, either addressing the person directly or speaking to their spirit if they are absent or no longer alive. Each phrase is simple yet heartfelt: "I honor the light within you," "I acknowledge our shared path," or "May our spirits find peace." Through these words, the practitioner seeks not to alter the past but to heal its impact on the present, cultivating a heart space free of resentment or regret.

To continue this heart-opening process, the practice of Compassionate Presence is introduced. This exercise is designed to expand the practitioner's capacity to sit in silence with others' pain, a skill that Gnostics believe deepens their own divine connection. In Compassionate Presence, the practitioner simply listens without interrupting or offering advice. By creating a safe space for another's story or suffering, they allow the heart's natural empathy to guide them. This presence becomes a living prayer of compassion, enabling the practitioner to connect deeply without judgment, nurturing a shared humanity. Through this practice, they develop an ability to meet others as equal reflections of the divine, learning to honor every person's journey with patience and humility.

The Path of the Heart also introduces the Heart-Centered Visualization, a guided practice for reinforcing the unity of all beings within the practitioner's heart. In this visualization, the practitioner pictures a single point of light within their heart, from which extends a network of radiant threads reaching out to every being. Each thread represents an unbreakable connection to others, forming a vast, interconnected web that pulses with the rhythm of divine love. With each breath, the practitioner imagines sending warmth, compassion, and healing along these threads, visualizing the energy flowing to those who may be suffering, lost, or in need of solace. This visualization cultivates a deep sense of shared purpose and connection, reinforcing the practitioner's role as an anchor of divine love.

In this chapter, Heart-Centered Mantra Meditation is used to anchor this energy of compassion within the practitioner's daily life. The mantra may be a sacred phrase from Gnostic texts or a simple affirmation like, "I am love; I am light." As they repeat this mantra, the practitioner allows the words to settle in the heart center, each repetition strengthening the heart's ability to express love freely and unconditionally. This meditative repetition helps transmute any residual barriers into pure, radiant energy, aligning their spirit with the divine.

The Practice of Daily Gratitude further nurtures the heart's expansion by training it to recognize and appreciate the sacred in all experiences. Each day, the practitioner dedicates a few moments to acknowledging three or more instances of beauty, kindness, or grace they encountered. They can write these reflections in a journal or simply recount them in quiet meditation. Gnostic wisdom teaches that gratitude creates a continuous flow of abundance within the heart, attuning it to divine presence in every moment. Through this awareness, the practitioner deepens their connection to life, seeing each experience as an opportunity for growth and love.

At the culmination of these practices, the practitioner is invited to the Ritual of Devotional Offering, a final act of surrender and unity with the divine. Here, they may offer a simple item—a flower, a piece of fruit, or a candle—to their sacred space as a symbolic gesture of their journey. Holding the object, the practitioner reflects on how their heart has transformed, giving thanks for the strength to forgive, the courage to love, and the wisdom to serve. As they place the offering on the altar, they state a personal intention or prayer, committing to live as an instrument of divine love. In Gnostic tradition, this ritual affirms that the heart, once awakened and purified, becomes a bridge to higher knowledge and a sanctuary for divine presence.

Through these advanced practices, the Path of the Heart unfolds as a transformative journey from self-love to universal love, from personal healing to cosmic connection. This chapter guides practitioners to a profound realization: that within each of us lies an infinite well of compassion, a reflection of the divine love that binds all beings. With every step on this path, the heart is not only healed but elevated, becoming a channel through which the divine flows freely, blessing both the practitioner and the world around them.

Chapter 25
Gnostic Magic

Gnostic magic invites the practitioner into a realm where the seen and unseen unite through intention, ritual, and the powerful connection to hidden wisdom. This form of magic differs from other traditions by seeking not the manipulation of the world, but alignment with divine knowledge and the forces of the inner self. Gnostic magic becomes a bridge between the physical and spiritual worlds, and here, it opens to those willing to approach it with reverence, clarity, and self-awareness.

The foundation of Gnostic magic begins with the practice of Conscious Invocation. Unlike simple recitations, invocations within the Gnostic tradition are calls to higher energies and entities rooted in the practitioner's spiritual path. The aim is not to summon, but to align. One might invoke Sophia, the embodiment of divine wisdom, or the Logos, symbolizing the ultimate truth. These invocations begin by creating a dedicated space, ideally a small altar adorned with symbols significant to the practitioner—whether it's a candle, an ancient symbol, or a crystal. The practitioner speaks with intention, visualizing the energy of the entity or archetype filling the space with presence and guidance. This focus brings their energies into harmony with the essence of the archetype, creating a heightened state of awareness.

A further, practical aspect of Gnostic magic is the use of Symbolic Gestures, also called mudras or sacred hand movements. Each gesture channels specific energies; for example, the open hand with the palm facing outward invokes protection, while hands pressed together at the heart center signal devotion and unity. When coupled with clear visualization and intent, these gestures act as silent calls, aligning the practitioner's physical and energetic self with their desired outcomes. In Gnostic practice, symbolic gestures represent not only personal intentions but universal principles, reminding practitioners of their alignment with divine forces.

Another potent aspect of Gnostic magic lies in the Creation of Talismans. Talismans are physical objects that hold and amplify specific intentions, often created during ritual and consecrated with prayer or invocation. The creation process demands deep focus; the practitioner may inscribe symbols, words, or even short prayers onto the talisman—each symbol drawn with intentional energy and meaning. The practitioner's intention is the heart of the talisman, linking it with the divine for continuous support and protection. Common materials for talismans in Gnosticism are gemstones, metals, and natural elements, each chosen for their symbolic properties. For instance, a quartz crystal might be chosen for clarity, while silver may be used for protection and receptivity to spiritual messages. These talismans are often carried or placed in sacred spaces, serving as reminders of one's ongoing spiritual alignment.

The practice of Sacred Incantation is another cornerstone of Gnostic magic. Here, practitioners use specific words or sounds believed to carry spiritual potency. These sounds often reflect ancient languages, such as Greek or Coptic, or personalized sounds that resonate with the practitioner's experience of the divine. When vocalized in the context of ritual, they transcend ordinary speech, becoming vibrational keys to heightened awareness. Each repetition of an incantation reinforces its meaning, slowly resonating within the practitioner, opening their consciousness to subtle insights or messages from their higher self.

In alignment with these practices, Visualization serves as an essential tool for manifesting intention within Gnostic magic. Unlike ordinary visualization, this technique relies on conjuring clear mental imagery of a desired outcome in sync with divine will. By closing their eyes and entering a state of focused calm, the practitioner visualizes their intention as already fulfilled, allowing this image to grow vivid in the mind's eye. Accompanying this image with a symbol—a bright light, a doorway, or a tree—adds an additional layer of potency, as symbols function as universal anchors within the spiritual subconscious.

To ensure a balanced approach to these practices, The Ritual of Grounding is advised after each session of Gnostic magic. Here, grounding ensures that the energies invoked in ritual are harmoniously integrated within the practitioner. This grounding practice might involve simple, mindful breathing, the visualization of roots connecting them to the earth, or holding a grounding object, such as a stone or piece of wood. By connecting with the earth, the practitioner safely disperses any remaining energies, balancing their physical and spiritual energies.

Lastly, practitioners of Gnostic magic often conclude their rituals with a Moment of Silence, a gesture of respect and alignment with the universe. In this silence, the practitioner allows the ritual's energy to settle within them, letting go of all remaining attachments to the outcome. This act of surrender symbolizes trust in divine wisdom, acknowledging that, beyond all intentions, the true power lies in unity with the greater whole.

Through each of these practices, Gnostic magic reveals itself as a path of intentional alignment and spiritual clarity. Far from seeking control, the practitioner aims to dissolve the barriers between the self and the divine, harnessing magic as a means of insight, empowerment, and profound inner harmony.

In deepening the practice of Gnostic magic, the practitioner ventures beyond foundational rituals to cultivate an intricate relationship with sacred symbols, mystical invocations, and the subtle, unseen energies that guide transformative experiences. Here, magic unfolds as a dialogue with the divine, bringing forth rituals of protection, manifestation, and revelation, each designed to open doors to the unseen realms and foster spiritual evolution. This chapter explores advanced techniques that enable the practitioner to harness these potent energies with awareness and respect, refining their path through intentional connection and sacred discipline.

At the heart of advanced Gnostic magic is the Ritual of Manifestation, a focused ceremony aimed at drawing from the divine wellspring to influence reality through will and alignment. In this ritual, practitioners bring forth their intentions with precision, beginning by setting a sacred space imbued with symbols of both their higher purpose and the specific goal they seek to manifest. Candles, chosen colors, and meaningful objects act as focal points, grounding the intention in the material realm. The practitioner enters a meditative state, visualizing the desired outcome in vivid, sacred imagery, then chants a mantra or invocation linked to this vision. Through repetition and mental clarity, the envisioned goal becomes more than a wish—it aligns with divine intention and unfolds in the practitioner's awareness as a reality already in motion.

A significant addition to these practices is the Invocation of Protective Forces, a ritual drawing upon Gnostic deities, archetypal symbols, and celestial entities to strengthen spiritual resilience and safeguard against discordant influences. In this advanced invocation, the practitioner consciously directs energy to form a protective barrier, visualized as a luminous shield or sphere. Symbols such as the ouroboros—a serpent or dragon eating its own tail, symbolizing wholeness—may be drawn or visualized around the practitioner, representing cyclical protection and the continuity of divine life. This protective ritual concludes with a grounding element, such as the placement of a protective stone or the marking of a sacred symbol on the skin or clothing, creating a tangible reminder of the protection invoked.

A further, more complex ritual in the Gnostic tradition is the Sacred Circle of Manifestation. This circle is not simply a physical arrangement but a living energetic construct that holds and amplifies the practitioner's intentions. Here, the practitioner arranges meaningful objects or symbolic representations in a circular formation, each item corresponding to specific qualities or energies they seek to invoke, such as strength, wisdom, or peace. The circle represents unity, connecting the individual's personal energies to the greater whole, enhancing each symbol's potency. As the practitioner stands within or faces the circle, they engage in a meditative state, envisioning these energies joining together to fulfill their intention. The circle remains undisturbed until the manifestation process completes, signifying the continuity of intent.

Building on the idea of manifestation, The Ritual of Cosmic Alignment is a practice that extends one's awareness beyond personal desire to harmonize with universal cycles and rhythms. This ritual, often performed under the influence of significant celestial events—such as full moons, equinoxes, or solstices—seeks to bring the practitioner's intentions into resonance with the cosmic forces. The practitioner selects a specific time and day according to these alignments, then begins with an invocation to the celestial energies present, acknowledging their role in the grand design. Guided by this acknowledgment, they perform visualizations, mantras, or offerings, connecting their consciousness to the patterns of the cosmos, allowing their intentions to flow harmoniously with natural cycles.

Another significant technique within advanced Gnostic magic is The Rite of Veiled Truths, a practice aimed at unveiling hidden wisdom. The practitioner enters this rite in a state of pure receptivity, emptying the mind of expectation or preconception. This ritual typically involves the creation of a darkened, silent space, allowing the individual to sink into profound silence and mystery. With closed eyes, the practitioner envisions themselves enveloped by a veil—a symbol of all that is hidden. As they slowly, deliberately move through a breathing pattern, the veil becomes increasingly thin, revealing flashes of insight, symbols, or images from deeper realms. To conclude, the practitioner journals any insights received, translating these veiled truths into awareness that may guide their future practices or decisions.

Alongside these ritual techniques, The Practice of Symbolic Language sharpens the practitioner's intuition, enabling them to interpret and use symbols as living representations of mystical realities. This practice involves meditation upon a symbol—such as the cross, spiral, or tree of life—allowing the practitioner to perceive the symbol as more than an abstract form, seeing it as a doorway into a particular quality of divine knowledge. The practitioner meditates upon the symbol, visualizing it in detail, sensing its energy and noticing any thoughts or images that arise. Over time, symbols become not only familiar but reveal layers of meaning, guiding the practitioner's spiritual evolution and serving as powerful tools in ritual work.

The Art of Astral Projection within Gnostic magic provides an advanced technique for exploring spiritual realms. The practitioner begins by lying comfortably, entering a deeply relaxed state, and focusing on the sensation of lightness in the body. Through breathwork and focused visualization, they imagine themselves floating above their physical form, mentally reciting mantras or intentions as they project their awareness beyond the confines of the material body. This form of projection is approached with caution and respect, as it exposes the practitioner to various planes of existence, allowing glimpses of knowledge inaccessible in ordinary states. Upon return, grounding techniques such as conscious breathing or visualizing roots into the earth ensure a balanced reintegration into the physical realm.

As Gnostic magic unfolds in these deeper practices, the practitioner understands that true power lies in reverent alignment rather than in control. Each ritual and invocation serves as a bridge to divine understanding, revealing that within these sacred acts lies a journey not merely of outward manifestation, but of profound self-discovery. The journey of Gnostic magic is, above all, one of respectful partnership with the sacred forces, each step a reminder of the limitless depths of consciousness and the mysteries woven into the fabric of existence.

Chapter 26
Integration of the Sacred

The journey into Gnosticism becomes complete only when the sacred flows seamlessly into everyday life, revealing how each moment, no matter how mundane, is imbued with divine significance. Integration of the sacred involves perceiving every action, thought, and interaction as a potential ritual, transforming the practitioner's entire experience into a living tapestry of spirituality. Here, the boundaries between the spiritual and the physical dissolve, allowing the practitioner to live in constant communion with the divine. This chapter opens pathways to cultivating a reverent life, where devotion becomes a steady undercurrent within every routine.

This form of integration begins with Mindful Presence, a practice where the practitioner approaches each day with heightened awareness and conscious participation. This presence is not only a passive observation but an active recognition of the sacred. When making daily choices—whether in conversation, work, or even in solitude—the practitioner pauses to acknowledge the significance of each action. The simple act of breathing becomes an invocation, the practice of being present as a gesture of devotion. By focusing attention on the details of each moment, the practitioner taps into the energy within them, bringing a sense of wonder to all aspects of life.

Another essential practice is Sacred Ritualization of Daily Routines, transforming activities like eating, bathing, and even commuting into moments of communion. Eating, for instance, becomes a ritual when approached with gratitude and intention.

By pausing to offer silent thanks, one connects with the spirit of nourishment and the life force inherent in food. This gratitude is not limited to words; it is felt deeply, recognizing the interconnected web of existence that brought this meal to life. Bathing, too, is imbued with sacredness by visualizing the cleansing of not only the body but also the energy field, symbolizing renewal. This ritualization elevates simple acts into ceremonies of spiritual significance.

Incorporating Morning and Evening Devotions is another way of rooting the sacred into daily life. Morning devotion might include a simple mantra, prayer, or visualization to set the day's intention, inviting the practitioner's higher self to guide their actions and thoughts. Likewise, in the evening, reflecting on the day with gratitude becomes an opportunity to acknowledge lessons learned and to close the day with a sense of peace. A candle, incense, or soft chanting can be used to mark the beginning and end of each day, encapsulating these rituals in a tangible, sensory experience that reinforces the boundary between the sacred space within and the external world.

The Practice of Gratitude anchors this integration, reminding the practitioner of their connection to everything. Gratitude here goes beyond acknowledgment; it becomes a language, a way to engage with each aspect of life meaningfully. By developing a gratitude practice—whether through a daily journal, quiet reflections, or intentional affirmations—the practitioner learns to see beauty and purpose even in difficult moments. Each challenge becomes a teacher, every gift a reminder of life's abundance. The practitioner can deepen this practice by offering thanks for events and experiences that typically go unnoticed, gradually expanding their awareness of the infinite ways the divine manifests.

Living with sacred awareness also requires Compassionate Interaction, an approach where each person encountered is viewed as an expression of the divine. This level of compassion arises from understanding that everyone is on their own spiritual journey, often navigating challenges unseen. The practitioner listens attentively, speaks thoughtfully, and acts with empathy, recognizing their role as a vessel of the divine in their interactions. Compassion becomes a means of honoring the interconnectedness of all beings, and every interaction is transformed into an opportunity for spiritual practice. Each moment spent with another person becomes a reflection of unity and a chance to deepen the integration of the sacred.

To cultivate a life fully infused with spirituality, the practitioner may also observe Seasons and Cycles, aligning their personal rhythm with the natural world. Recognizing the cyclical patterns of the moon, seasons, and elements, the practitioner honors their connection to the cosmos and the divine order within. By noting how energy shifts with these cycles—such as the renewal of spring or the introspection of winter—they learn to harmonize their own actions with these natural flows, embracing times of growth, release, and introspection. Rituals can be adapted to these cycles, such as planting intentions during new moons or reflecting on personal growth during full moons, strengthening the sense of oneness with all creation.

Alongside these practices, Reverence for the Elements becomes a daily observance, where earth, water, fire, and air are acknowledged as the building blocks of both the physical and spiritual worlds. This reverence might manifest in small rituals, like lighting a candle to honor fire, watering plants with awareness of the life-giving nature of water, or walking barefoot on the ground to connect with the earth. These gestures build a relationship with each element, cultivating respect and drawing on their energies to nurture the spirit. Practitioners may find that these moments of connection awaken a deeper understanding of the elements' roles in balancing and enriching their own lives.

To fully integrate the sacred, Personal Reflection becomes an essential component, allowing the practitioner to explore how their journey aligns with their inner truth. Regular self-reflection—through journaling, contemplation, or dialogue with the higher self—enables a continual process of alignment, realignment, and growth. This inner dialogue helps clarify values, renew intentions, and identify ways to deepen the sense of unity with the divine in all aspects of life. Reflection also reveals any obstacles to living a sacred life, providing guidance on overcoming inner resistance and enhancing alignment with the spiritual path.

Lastly, the sacred integration is reinforced by Acts of Service, where the practitioner extends their devotion outward, contributing to others' well-being as a direct expression of their inner alignment. Service here is not an obligation but an offering, a way to express gratitude for the gifts of consciousness and connection. Small acts of kindness, intentional support, or community involvement are seen as extensions of spiritual practice, grounded in the understanding that every being is an aspect of the divine. Each act of service reaffirms the practitioner's place in the web of existence, bridging the inner journey with the outer world.

Through these practices, Gnosticism transcends individual rituals and meditations, infusing life itself with reverence and meaning. Each moment, choice, and encounter becomes an invitation to deepen one's connection to the divine essence. As practitioners integrate the sacred into their lives, they find that the boundaries between the physical and spiritual dissolve, creating a seamless experience of unity and presence. This living spirituality shapes each day, filling it with purpose, joy, and a profound sense of peace that blossoms from within, reflecting the divine light into every facet of existence.

The path to a life fully infused with sacred awareness deepens as the practitioner embraces subtle yet transformative practices that weave spirituality seamlessly into the fabric of existence. In this second part, the sacred becomes not just a series of mindful acts but a lens through which the practitioner perceives the entirety of life. Ritual and reality meld, illuminating each moment with reverence. In cultivating such a state, the practitioner's awareness radiates a grounded yet transcendent spirit, allowing the divine to permeate the mundane. As integration progresses, the simple becomes profound, and the complex dissolves into unity.

The integration deepens through Rituals of Thresholds, which acknowledge life's transitions as spiritual gateways. Waking, sleeping, leaving home, or beginning new projects—all are marked by small rituals that honor these thresholds. For example, upon waking, the practitioner may touch the earth, setting an intention of grounded clarity for the day. Before leaving the house, they might pause, visualizing a protective light surrounding them. These practices extend to the beginning of creative or professional tasks, where lighting a candle or saying a silent blessing allows each activity to flow with purpose and aligned energy. In recognizing these thresholds, the practitioner heightens their sensitivity to life's sacred rhythm, where each transition becomes a reverent moment of intention.

To cultivate continual awareness, the practitioner delves into Conscious Breathing Techniques, using the breath to anchor their presence in each experience. Conscious breathing, unlike controlled or forced breathing, emphasizes a gentle, unbroken awareness that flows with each inhale and exhale. This breathwork can be applied in various moments, whether during conversations, creative tasks, or periods of solitude, to foster a steady connection to the present. The breath becomes an instrument of focus, aligning the practitioner's inner and outer worlds. This practice trains the mind to remain in the here and now, dissolving distractions and promoting a sense of continuity in the sacred.

The practice of Blessing the Mundane amplifies integration further, transforming routine acts into rituals of gratitude and connection. Every task, whether washing dishes, organizing a workspace, or tending to plants, becomes an opportunity to engage fully with the present and honor its significance. As they bless each action with mindful attention, the practitioner infuses their day with a heightened awareness of purpose and beauty. This process of blessing—performed in silence or with intentional words—helps transcend the notion of separation, uniting the practitioner with their surroundings in a shared spiritual exchange.

Heart-Centered Living becomes central, where decisions, responses, and perspectives are drawn from the intuitive intelligence of the heart. This practice expands the initial concepts of gratitude and compassion by aligning them with a deep, continuous connection to the heart. Living from this space encourages the practitioner to interpret the world through an empathetic, open lens, understanding that the heart possesses a wisdom that transcends intellect. Each interaction with others, each response to events, is filtered through this heart-centered awareness, fostering harmony and resonance in all relationships and engagements.

Sacred Symbolism finds a place in this journey, where symbols that resonate with the practitioner's spiritual path are consciously woven into daily life. Whether through clothing adorned with meaningful symbols, carrying a small emblem of protection, or decorating one's environment with objects of spiritual resonance, these symbols serve as silent guides, reminders of the practitioner's inner path. The presence of such symbols, chosen intentionally, reinforces their purpose and sustains their connection to the divine. Over time, they come to represent not only protection or wisdom but a continuous link to the practitioner's commitment to live a sacred life.

Another vital aspect of integration is Seasonal and Lunar Attunement, an advanced approach that builds on the awareness of natural cycles. By aligning personal practices with the rhythms of the earth and moon, the practitioner deepens their sense of harmony with larger cosmic forces. For example, a new moon may signal a time for setting intentions, while a full moon provides an opportunity for reflection and release. Likewise, the solstices and equinoxes mark points of transformation, where specific rituals can honor shifts within and around the practitioner. This alignment fosters an intuitive flow, where personal growth mirrors natural cycles, embedding the practitioner's spiritual evolution in the vast rhythms of existence.

With these practices, Reflective Solitude gains prominence, urging the practitioner to spend intentional time in silence and contemplation. Unlike earlier meditative practices, this solitude involves a more profound encounter with stillness, a willingness to listen without expectation. In reflective solitude, one may take long walks in nature, meditate without a specific focus, or engage in silent creative activities. This practice acts as a bridge between structured spiritual practice and unstructured receptivity, allowing insights and divine connections to emerge naturally. In this silence, the practitioner hears the subtle call of their true self, which guides them in deeper integration.

Furthermore, Mindful Technology Use becomes a cornerstone of sacred living, especially in a modern context. The practitioner consciously limits distractions, curating digital consumption with the same care applied to physical surroundings. This approach ensures that technology serves the practitioner's growth rather than disrupting it. Intentional pauses from screens, specific time blocks for focused interaction with digital tools, and designated device-free periods cultivate a harmonious relationship with technology. This balance allows the practitioner to engage with technology while remaining anchored in their spiritual values, fostering a life that honors presence and clarity.

Integrating the sacred also invites Communal Spirituality, an intentional approach to connecting with others who share or support one's path. Rather than seeing the spiritual journey as a solitary pursuit, communal spirituality enriches integration by offering shared experiences, collective rituals, and mutual support. The practitioner may engage in group meditations, participate in community gatherings, or collaborate on service projects. Each communal encounter becomes an opportunity for growth, support, and the shared resonance of collective energy. Through such gatherings, the practitioner strengthens their understanding of unity, finding companionship in the collective exploration of the divine.

The chapter concludes with a focus on Radical Presence, a practice that requires a profound level of awareness in each moment. Unlike earlier forms of presence, radical presence demands the practitioner's full engagement, leaving no room for inner or outer distractions. This presence, unwavering and complete, unveils the deepest layers of experience. By embodying radical presence, the practitioner steps into a space where duality dissipates, leaving only the vibrant pulse of the sacred. In this state, every word, every gesture, and every breath is an act of devotion, a testament to the infinite unity that underlies existence.

This advanced integration of the sacred transforms Gnosticism from a set of practices into a way of life. Every facet of existence becomes a reflection of the divine, illuminating the path not only as a journey but as the destination itself. The practitioner moves through life as a vessel of light, carrying the sacred into every corner of existence, embracing the mystery and magnificence of a world where nothing is separate from the divine essence.

Chapter 27
Practice of Service

Service stands as a central pillar of the Gnostic journey, embodying the transition from inward revelation to outward action, from the mysteries of self-knowledge to the manifestations of compassion in the world. In the context of Gnosticism, service transcends the traditional view of duty; it is not simply an obligation but a profound channel for transformation and connection with others. Through service, the practitioner transforms inner wisdom into compassionate acts that dissolve barriers between self and other, illuminating the interconnectedness of all life. This chapter introduces the essential principles and practices of Gnostic service, unveiling it as both an offering and a pathway to higher consciousness.

The practice of service within Gnosticism begins with cultivating Empathetic Awareness, a heightened sensitivity to the needs and emotions of those around us. This awareness goes beyond intellectual understanding; it demands a deep, heartfelt connection that resonates with the essence of another being. Through meditative practices that foster empathy, such as silent visualization exercises, the practitioner learns to connect with others' suffering and joys without judgment or projection. In this way, service becomes an expression of one's own sacred nature, responding to the soul's call to heal and uplift, not through duty, but through a natural extension of love.

Listening with Presence forms the first practical layer of service, emphasizing an active and attentive engagement with those seeking guidance or support. In this practice, the practitioner learns to quiet their mind and simply be present, holding space without interruption, interpretation, or advice. This sacred listening allows others to feel seen and valued on their journey, helping them explore their own truths and discover answers within themselves. Listening as service aligns with Gnostic principles by facilitating inner revelation rather than imposing external beliefs. Here, the practitioner embodies the archetype of the guide, nurturing transformation through presence alone.

To deepen this approach, the practitioner explores Energetic Healing Techniques, bringing light and calm to those around them without speaking a word. Simple visualizations of surrounding others with protective light, sending healing energy, or practicing silent blessings cultivate an atmosphere of peace and safety for everyone in one's environment. By practicing these techniques with intentionality, the practitioner becomes a conduit for healing energies, radiating calm that helps others attune to their own center. Energetic healing is done humbly and with reverence, as the practitioner does not assume the role of healer but instead allows divine energy to flow through, respecting the recipient's free will and personal journey.

In embracing the path of service, Selfless Action becomes a guiding principle. Unlike actions driven by a desire for personal recognition or reward, selfless service asks the practitioner to set aside the ego's attachments, focusing entirely on the benefit of others. Selfless action may involve small acts of kindness, thoughtful gestures, or significant sacrifices, yet in each instance, the intent remains pure—untouched by expectation. This form of action aligns deeply with the Gnostic journey, as it requires the practitioner to move beyond the self and resonate with a deeper, collective soul. It becomes a subtle yet powerful practice in dissolving illusions of separateness, revealing each act of service as a direct encounter with the divine.

As the practitioner advances, Guided Compassionate Support offers another layer of service, one that combines wisdom with empathy. This aspect of Gnostic service encourages the practitioner to guide those who seek spiritual understanding without leading or imposing. Compassionate support may involve sharing insights, asking reflective questions, or offering perspective when invited. This practice respects each person's autonomy, allowing them to remain the architect of their spiritual path. In this way, the practitioner's guidance becomes a gentle nudge rather than a directive, reinforcing Gnostic values of self-discovery and inner sovereignty.

Material Service—offering resources, time, and tangible assistance—is another potent way to ground spiritual principles in everyday life. The practitioner contributes to the welfare of others in a direct and immediate manner, whether through charitable donations, volunteering, or simply helping with daily tasks. This form of service has an immediate impact, as it alleviates physical or emotional burdens and creates space for those assisted to find their own spiritual growth. Material service, approached with humility and integrity, transforms each act into a sacrament, where helping another is an acknowledgment of shared humanity and divine essence.

To maintain equilibrium, Reflective Boundaries are essential within service. The practitioner learns to serve without depletion by recognizing personal limits and maintaining practices that sustain their own well-being. Reflective boundaries do not imply separation; rather, they are an act of respect for both the practitioner and those they serve, ensuring that service is given from a place of fullness rather than sacrifice. Practices such as grounding, mindful withdrawal, and energy protection serve as reminders that true service thrives not from self-neglect but from balanced, sustainable compassion.

Service, at its core, becomes a Sacred Offering, a gift from the spirit rather than a task of obligation. In this way, it is deeply aligned with Gnostic principles, where each act reflects a deeper resonance with divine purpose. Simple acts of service—whether offering a word of encouragement, sharing knowledge, or giving without expectation—are performed as offerings to the divine presence within each person, cultivating a world that reveres the sacred in all beings. The practitioner begins to view every interaction, every exchange, as a moment of divine service, infusing life itself with sacred intention.

The chapter concludes with Silent Service, a form of service where the practitioner acts anonymously, allowing the impact to remain unseen. In this practice, the act is given freely, without attachment to outcome or recognition. Silent service, such as leaving a gift for a stranger, cleaning a shared space without mention, or sending blessings silently, represents the purest form of service. It liberates the practitioner from ego and expectation, immersing them in the joy of giving as an act of love. In silent service, the practitioner embraces the ultimate form of surrender, where giving itself becomes a path to unity with the divine.

In these practices, Gnostic service emerges not only as a way to uplift others but as an invitation to dissolve the barriers between the self and the greater whole. The practitioner discovers that through acts of genuine service, they not only support others but encounter the divine presence in every being and every moment. Through this journey, the boundaries of self are softened, and service becomes a vehicle for transcending separateness, embodying love, and experiencing the Gnostic vision of unity within the world.

Having cultivated the foundational principles of service, the practitioner now deepens this path by embracing more structured, transformative acts that uplift not only individuals but the broader community of seekers. This chapter guides the practitioner through advanced forms of service, including leading healing practices, facilitating group meditations, and fostering spaces of collective support. Here, service shifts from a personal practice to one that harmonizes the community, creating channels through which the divine flows to all.

The journey begins with the practice of Group Healing, where the practitioner learns to conduct healing sessions that tap into the collective energy of a group. Unlike individual healing, which focuses solely on one recipient, group healing allows the practitioner to work with multiple energies, connecting participants in a shared experience of renewal. Before initiating group healing, the practitioner sets a clear intention and leads the group through grounding techniques to create a unified field of energy. Visualizations, invocations of light, or gentle chanting guide each participant into resonance, allowing divine energy to flow freely among them. This sacred circle magnifies the power of healing, demonstrating that true service in Gnosticism reaches beyond personal boundaries into shared consciousness.

The chapter then explores Guided Meditation Leadership. By leading others through meditation, the practitioner acts as a bridge, helping participants transcend ordinary awareness and connect with higher realms. As a meditation guide, the practitioner nurtures a safe, calming environment, offering gentle verbal cues to ease participants into deeper states. Through a combination of visualization, silence, and soft guiding, the leader offers each participant a direct encounter with their own inner essence. This role, approached with humility, is one of profound service, as it enables each person to touch a part of themselves that often lies hidden, granting glimpses of the divine within.

Creating Gnostic Study Groups becomes another advanced form of service. By establishing or nurturing study groups, the practitioner offers a space where seekers can delve into Gnostic texts, discuss spiritual insights, and support each other's growth. In facilitating such gatherings, the practitioner encourages open, respectful dialogue, honoring each participant's unique understanding and perspective. This communal learning environment enriches each individual's journey, as shared insights ignite new realizations and encourage deeper introspection. The study group becomes a living expression of Gnostic wisdom, where knowledge transforms into lived experience, and each member grows within the collective light.

The practice of Spiritual Mentorship allows the practitioner to offer one-on-one guidance, fostering an environment where others feel safe to explore their spiritual questions and challenges. Acting as a mentor requires both patience and intuition, as the practitioner learns to listen deeply and respond in ways that honor the mentee's unique path. Mentorship in the Gnostic tradition emphasizes the inner teacher rather than external advice, so the mentor's role is to gently guide each seeker towards their own insights. Through reflective dialogue, storytelling, or silent presence, the mentor assists others in uncovering truths that already reside within. This intimate form of service is transformative, illuminating the Gnostic path for both mentor and mentee.

As service within the Gnostic path intensifies, the practitioner embraces Group Rituals of Unity and Healing. These rituals are designed to harmonize the collective energy of the group, creating a shared experience that amplifies each individual's connection to the divine. The practitioner may incorporate elements such as synchronized breathing, chanting, or the use of symbols and sacred objects. By leading the group through intentional gestures, invocations, and shared blessings, the practitioner helps to dissolve individual separateness, allowing each participant to experience a unified field of consciousness. Through these rituals, the group collectively resonates with the divine, discovering a profound sense of interconnectedness that transcends words.

To maintain the integrity of service, the practitioner explores Ethical Boundaries and Spiritual Discernment. As service becomes more complex, it becomes crucial to practice discernment, ensuring that guidance and energy shared with others align with the highest intentions. Ethical boundaries protect both the practitioner and those served, fostering respect and preserving each person's free will. This discernment requires an awareness of personal motivations, a commitment to humility, and an unwavering dedication to serving the divine essence within all beings. Ethical service also involves recognizing when one's energy is depleted or when certain guidance is best left to others. Through discernment, the practitioner refines their role as a servant of light, always mindful of acting from a place of pure intention.

Creating Sacred Spaces for Community Healing becomes a culminating act of service, transforming physical spaces into realms where the divine presence is palpable. Whether in a private home, an outdoor sanctuary, or a dedicated spiritual center, the practitioner learns to consecrate spaces with intention, imbuing them with peace, protection, and sacred energy. Techniques such as purifying the space with herbs, invoking light through visualization, or arranging symbols that resonate with Gnostic archetypes turn ordinary spaces into sacred sites. This practice is one of quiet power, as it enables others to feel the calm and sacredness of the environment, enhancing their connection to the divine and easing their own path toward healing.

Finally, the chapter introduces the concept of Unconditional Service, where acts of kindness and guidance are offered with complete detachment from outcome or recognition. Unconditional service is not merely a practice but a state of being, where the practitioner becomes a vessel through which the divine serves itself. In this state, each gesture, word, or moment of listening is given freely, without attachment to how it is received. The practitioner transcends the personal self, experiencing service as a natural flow of the divine presence. Acts such as anonymous giving, silent blessings, and unseen support become the ultimate expressions of Gnostic service, where the practitioner surrenders fully to the unfolding of the divine plan, trusting that each act aligns with the greater good.

Through these practices, the path of service deepens, and the practitioner becomes a channel of divine grace within the community. This advanced service brings the practitioner into a profound communion with the Gnostic ideal of unity, as each act becomes a step towards dissolving the boundaries of individual existence. The group healing, mentorship, sacred space creation, and unconditional service elevate both the giver and receiver, weaving each participant into the divine fabric of life itself. The journey of service thus fulfills its sacred purpose—not merely to uplift others but to reveal the ever-present, unbroken connection that unites all beings in the divine.

Chapter 28
Spiritual Ascension

Spiritual ascension, as envisioned in the Gnostic path, emerges not as a goal to be conquered but as an unfolding, a rising out of the ordinary, like mist lifting from the earth. Ascension becomes an essential part of Gnostic practice, a transformation rooted in detachment and union with the divine—a movement beyond self and form, stepping into realms not bound by flesh, name, or the habitual demands of ego. Here, the practice converges on the integration of all knowledge and inner experiences, leading the practitioner toward an encounter with the divine, in which nothing is lost and all is found.

This stage of ascension is woven from a tapestry of previous practices, each strand contributing to the wholeness of the seeker's spirit. Gnostic ascension involves the harmonizing of the soul's light with the infinite, detaching from attachments not by negating them but by transmuting their significance. As the seeker approaches these final steps, the heart becomes the compass, moving beyond knowledge, touching a timeless essence within. It requires devotion to inner silence, constant mindfulness, and the elevation of each thought and action to one of sacred resonance.

In this ascension process, the chapter first delves into the Practice of Dissolution, where the practitioner begins to dissolve their sense of individuality. Not to abandon the self, but to transform it, so it merges seamlessly with the divine essence. Through visualization and focused meditation, the practitioner imagines boundaries of the self fading, every thought, emotion, and sensation merging with a field of pure, radiant light. This dissolution is a surrender, where each personal attachment is relinquished in the presence of something boundless. The ego loosens its grip as the practitioner's awareness expands into infinity, a dance of presence and release.

Next, The Art of Observing the Eternal Now becomes a key practice, allowing the seeker to recognize that all moments are contained in the present. By bringing deep awareness into each moment, the practitioner touches a timeless state, where worries, past regrets, and anticipations fade. There, in the stillness, lies a profound unity with the divine—a moment where all is known, not through the mind, but through direct experience. Each breath, heartbeat, and sensation becomes a sacred chant, anchoring the seeker into the eternal now. As this practice deepens, the layers of mundane reality begin to thin, and the seeker glimpses realms of light and wisdom, as if seeing the world through the eyes of the divine.

This journey also introduces Meditation on Divine Union, a contemplative practice focused on merging the practitioner's spirit with the Pleroma, the fullness of the divine. In this meditation, the practitioner moves beyond symbols and thoughts, inviting the essence of the divine into their very being. Words, desires, and thoughts are quieted; only the longing for unity remains. This meditation cultivates an unshakable connection with the divine, as each breath becomes a bridge between worlds. The seeker is taught to let the divine infuse every cell, every pulse, until the line between seeker and divine dissolves, creating a momentary unity that expands consciousness beyond the limits of individuality.

To deepen this state, Chanting the Silent Word is introduced. In Gnostic tradition, sound holds a key to ascension, yet here it is the silent word—the vibration felt rather than heard—that leads the practitioner beyond the veil of sound into the realm of pure frequency. The silent word is an inner chant, a vibration born from intent, pulsing through the heart and mind, guiding the soul toward alignment with the cosmos. By focusing on this vibration, the practitioner feels the inner shift toward a resonance that aligns with divine wisdom. Each silent utterance brings the practitioner closer to transcending the limitations of form, enhancing the experience of merging with the divine essence.

As ascension demands a lightness of spirit, The Practice of Pure Intention becomes essential. Here, the seeker refines their intentions, purifying each thought and action so it reflects the divine will rather than personal desire. This alignment with pure intention becomes a path of humility, where the practitioner surrenders personal motivations, allowing each moment to be an expression of the divine. Pure intention is cultivated through regular reflection, shedding any attachments to outcomes, and embracing each act as a form of devotion. As this purity of purpose becomes second nature, the practitioner's life aligns with the flow of the cosmos, and ascension becomes a natural, unfolding process rather than a destination.

In the ascension journey, The Vision of the Pleroma awaits those who persist. This is not a vision in the ordinary sense but a transcendental experience where the practitioner senses the vast, interconnected unity of all creation. Through advanced visualization, the practitioner's awareness expands, perceiving layers of reality from the dense material to realms of pure light. Each level reveals a unique aspect of the divine, showing the interplay of existence as both form and formlessness. The Pleroma encompasses all opposites, from dark to light, from finite to infinite, and the practitioner understands that these are not contradictions but aspects of a single, all-encompassing reality. Here, the self dissolves entirely into the fabric of being, a profound merging where all distinctions between seeker and divine vanish.

Preparation for Final Detachment begins, the ultimate step in this ascent. Through reflection and meditation, the practitioner is guided to relinquish even the most subtle attachments, recognizing that true ascension means releasing all to become a vessel for divine presence. This practice is an exercise in transcendence, where the practitioner moves beyond concepts, beliefs, and even the desire for enlightenment, entering a state of complete surrender. Final detachment is the threshold of ascension, where the seeker understands that they must relinquish all they know to enter the unknown.

In these practices, ascension becomes not a departure but an arrival, an unveiling of the divine essence within, revealing the practitioner as both a vessel of light and the light itself. Every practice, every breath, and every thought becomes an expression of this divine ascent, creating a resonance that permeates all life. Here, Gnostic ascension transforms the practitioner, as the self surrenders into the cosmic dance, merging with the divine fabric that unites all of creation.

At the pinnacle of spiritual ascension, the Gnostic path invites the practitioner to enter into a union that transcends form, language, and understanding—a transformative return to the divine, experienced as both end and beginning, the final dissolution and a rebirth into boundless consciousness. This stage draws upon the practices of purity, devotion, and transcendence, as the seeker steps beyond the dualities of self and other, beyond the temporal flow of past and future, and into the timeless expanse of the divine presence. Here, the deepest practices emerge, guiding the seeker to surrender into the mystery of divine union.

One of the core practices in this ultimate ascent is Breathing with the Divine Pulse. This technique aligns the practitioner's breath with the rhythm of the cosmos itself, transforming each inhalation into an invitation to the divine and each exhalation into an act of surrender. To begin, the seeker envisions their breath as a link between body and spirit, their pulse in harmony with the heartbeat of creation. By attuning to this rhythm, they start to perceive a universal frequency—a pulse of life that transcends individual identity and connects all beings. This breathing becomes an entry into the divine presence, quieting the mind and immersing the practitioner in a stillness that speaks to eternity.

In alignment with this is the Practice of Divine Silence, a profound state where words, thoughts, and the needs of the mind fall away entirely, and the practitioner rests in the silent awareness of existence itself. Divine silence is a space beyond meditation, an encounter with the void from which all creation emerges. The practitioner learns to hold this silence, allowing it to deepen with each session, until the mind surrenders its grasp on knowledge and relinquishes its search for answers. In this sacred silence, the divine reveals itself not as a concept, but as presence—an all-encompassing awareness in which the seeker dissolves, encountering the infinite without boundary or division.

Accompanying this silence is the Invocation of the Sacred Light, a meditative visualization where the practitioner envisions a sphere of light descending from the Pleroma to envelop them, flooding every cell with divine essence. This light, often visualized as brilliant, all-embracing, and pure, represents both the origin and the destination of the seeker's spiritual journey. As they breathe in this light, it begins to dissolve personal layers—fear, desire, and identity—leaving only the essence of spirit. This is not just an imagined light, but a felt presence, an intense vibration that opens pathways within, illuminating the divine spark that lies dormant within each being. In this light, the seeker becomes aware of their unity with all creation, a oneness beyond space and time.

Next, the chapter introduces The Sacred Union Meditation, a practice of merging with the divine through a symbolic and felt experience of becoming one with the universal life force. In this meditation, the practitioner is guided to visualize the divine as a presence surrounding and penetrating them, as if they are merging with an ocean of light, consciousness, and love. Each breath becomes a deeper surrender, and in each heartbeat, they feel the divine essence expanding, reaching into every layer of being until no separation remains. This meditation evokes an experience of the self as both wave and ocean, where the finite touches the infinite, and the seeker experiences a unity that transcends words or understanding.

A key aspect of this advanced stage is the Practice of Perennial Awareness, a technique that helps the practitioner remain connected to the divine presence in every waking moment. Through this practice, they learn to maintain a state of heightened awareness, seeing the sacred in each experience, no matter how ordinary. It involves frequent mindfulness exercises, grounding practices, and reminders of the sacred to cultivate an unbroken connection to the divine. Perennial awareness teaches the seeker that ascension is not only reached in moments of stillness or ritual but is also woven into the fabric of daily life, each moment a prayer, each breath a step on the path to divine union.

To sustain this connection, the chapter presents Ecstatic Prayer, an intense and personal expression of devotion, where the seeker calls to the divine with every fiber of their being. Ecstatic prayer is an abandonment of self into a state of deep longing, where the practitioner pours out their spirit, not in words alone but in a silent cry for unity. This prayer is less about supplication and more about merging, an invocation of oneness, where the practitioner allows their entire being to resonate with divine love. This ecstatic state can bring visions, insights, or simply a profound peace, as the practitioner aligns entirely with the sacred presence, experiencing ascension as a communion, a rapture beyond the confines of language.

As the ascension process unfolds, The Ritual of Final Release becomes a crucial rite, representing the practitioner's ultimate detachment from all that is known. This ritual is a symbolic gesture, where the seeker releases even the subtlest attachments—be they to self-identity, spiritual goals, or even the desire for enlightenment. In this ritual, each attachment is acknowledged, then offered to the divine in gratitude and surrender, until the practitioner stands in pure openness. The Final Release is a testament to faith and surrender, a readiness to dissolve into the unknown, trusting the divine to guide and hold all things.

Completing this journey is The Practice of Divine Embodiment, a state where the practitioner becomes not just a seeker but a vessel for the divine. Here, every word, action, and thought is permeated with the essence of the sacred, a radiant expression of ascended consciousness. Divine embodiment is a return to the world as a new being, seeing through the eyes of the soul, acting from the heart of the divine. In this state, the practitioner understands that ascension is not a final destination but an eternal unfolding, a movement into the heart of existence that continues beyond form, thought, or action. It is a state of eternal becoming, where the spirit exists in harmony with all of creation, embodying love, compassion, and wisdom with each breath.

In these advanced practices, spiritual ascension becomes a reality, not as an escape from the world but as an entry into its deepest truth. The seeker who reaches this stage has transcended the need for knowledge, for structure, for form. They live as an expression of the divine, a presence in the world that radiates peace and unity. Through breath, silence, and surrender, the practitioner becomes an instrument of the divine, a manifestation of the eternal light that illuminates all creation. Ascension, thus, is the gift of becoming—a journey back to the origin, where all things are one, and the divine pulse beats in every heart.

Chapter 29
Journey Synthesis

In the journey of spiritual discovery, there comes a time to look back, to gather fragments of understanding, and to see the threads of transformation woven through each step. This moment is not a conclusion but a place to pause, to contemplate the depth of what has been encountered and the extent of the inner landscape now illuminated. In Gnosticism, this act of synthesis is sacred—a practice that gives meaning to the seeker's experience, allowing them to see how each ritual, meditation, and teaching has worked together, creating a tapestry of self-discovery, a unified journey toward gnosis.

The seeker's path began with curiosity, a spark kindled by the mysteries of ancient teachings, by words that spoke of wisdom hidden beyond ordinary perception. They encountered the Gnostic Principles, foundational concepts that laid bare the structure of existence and the duality between spirit and matter. These teachings on the Demiurge, Sophia, and the Pleroma were not mere knowledge to be stored away but transformative ideas that altered how they perceived reality, setting a new lens through which to see the world. This foundation was essential, as it introduced them to the essence of the Gnostic path, to the understanding that liberation arises not from external dogma but from the light found within.

As they moved further, the seeker learned the art of Spiritual Preparation, a discipline that rooted them in a sacred practice of cleansing and reverence. Preparing mind, body, and spirit became a gateway, creating a purified space to welcome the wisdom that would unfold. Through rituals of protection, the establishment of a sacred space, and purification practices, the seeker learned the value of intention and respect. This preparation served as a continual reminder that the Gnostic journey is not one to be undertaken casually, but with a seriousness that acknowledges the profound nature of inner work.

With preparation complete, the seeker was guided into Gnostic Meditations, where the layers of thought and ego were set aside, and silence became a trusted companion. In this silence, a new awareness emerged, a realm of insight where knowledge of the self began to reveal itself. Through concentration and contemplation, they practiced the art of meeting their own mind, accessing a depth of consciousness previously hidden. These moments were more than exercises; they were glimpses into the profound simplicity of being, a practice that stripped away distractions, allowing the essence of gnosis to rise within.

The practice of Self-Analysis followed, challenging the seeker to go deeper still. This journey of reflection, of examining thoughts, emotions, and actions, was not without resistance. The seeker faced parts of themselves long obscured, habits and patterns that clung tightly, blocking the path forward. Yet, with each realization, with each insight gained, there was growth. The journal became a mirror, a canvas where the soul painted its stories, revealing patterns that were ready to be transformed. By understanding these personal threads, the seeker touched upon the core of transformation—a journey of knowing and freeing oneself from the limitations that bind.

Protection rituals, including energy shields and sacred symbols, took on new meaning as the seeker understood the importance of safeguarding the spiritual journey. These Protection Rituals were not simply for defense but were symbolic acts of devotion, of honoring the spirit within and maintaining an environment conducive to growth. The presence of the divine was invoked to create boundaries that honored both the journey and the inner light now beginning to shine brighter within the seeker.

A significant turn arrived with the alignment of Chakras and the discovery of energy centers that flowed within. Here, ancient Gnostic teachings met with the subtle energies of the body, as the seeker learned to perceive, balance, and nurture their own internal harmony. This experience was a revelation—a reminder that true gnosis encompasses the whole being, including the physical form, and that by aligning these centers, they would foster a state of unity, an embodiment of spiritual harmony.

The seeker also encountered Initiation Rituals, moments that marked profound shifts in their journey. Through these rites, they crossed thresholds, committing to deeper levels of understanding. Each initiation was a sacred bond, an act of surrender that acknowledged both humility and courage. These rites taught them that true transformation requires not only knowledge but a willingness to enter the unknown, to become the student again, seeking the wisdom of the spirit.

In Creative Visualization, the seeker discovered the power of imagination in manifesting spiritual goals, connecting with archetypal symbols, and opening new dimensions within. Visualization became a practice of creating reality, of attuning the mind to higher frequencies. These images were not merely pictures but bridges between the seen and unseen, a tool for accessing realms beyond the physical.

Through the practices of Spiritual Healing, the seeker engaged with the capacity to heal wounds both within and beyond, recognizing the body as a vessel for divine energy. In learning to align their being with higher vibrations, they discovered a connection to the universal force that brings harmony to the fragmented self. The healing journey was a reminder that the divine spark within is also a source of renewal and that through nurturing this connection, both self and others could experience wholeness.

By walking The Path of Wisdom, the seeker embraced the idea that wisdom is a lived experience, a quality woven into each day. In each interaction, every choice became a mirror for spiritual truth, a practice of embodying insight. Wisdom was no longer confined to books but became an active principle guiding the seeker toward inner truth.

In this first stage of synthesis, the seeker finds themselves transformed. Each chapter, each step, has built upon the last, creating a profound sense of connection. Now, as they pause to reflect, they see that every ritual, meditation, and introspection was a stepping stone, each part forming an intricate design, leading them to a deeper understanding of self, spirit, and the vast mystery of the divine. And while there remains much more to embrace in the journey, this moment of reflection is one of gratitude, of awareness that each step was a necessary unfolding—a path that ultimately leads back to the heart of gnosis itself.

As the seeker stands upon the threshold of completion, the journey's weight and wonder settle deeply into their being. There is a sense of culmination, yet a paradoxical understanding that this end is merely the beginning. The paths walked, the transformations undergone, and the moments of gnosis that have flickered through their consciousness now merge into a singular, profound awareness: the journey was always about becoming.

Every meditation, ritual, and introspection has served as both map and compass, guiding them into the uncharted territory of the self and beyond, into realms of the infinite. Each chapter woven together, from initial whispers of ancient teachings to the direct experience of divine presence, forms an inner architecture of wisdom. What was once fragmented knowledge, an assembly of practices and philosophies, now stands as a cohesive, living truth within the seeker's spirit.

This final stage invites them to look beyond the limitations of structured practice, for in the Gnostic way, true gnosis is a light that permeates the whole of life. The rituals, symbols, and tools become like well-worn guides, familiar yet expansive, always pointing inward. Now, the seeker recognizes that the path to the divine is not confined to sacred spaces or moments of stillness alone. Rather, it is found in each breath, every heartbeat—a steady rhythm that resonates with the cosmic pulse of the Pleroma, the fullness of divine reality.

Reflecting on the journey's early steps, the seeker recalls the foundational understanding of Gnostic principles. Concepts that once seemed abstract—the Demiurge, Sophia, the duality of spirit and matter—have transformed through lived experience. The journey showed that these ideas were not distant doctrines but mirrored the inner landscapes of the seeker's soul, embodying struggles, aspirations, and glimpses of divinity that now reside within.

There is also the realization of the intimate relationship built with the Higher Self, a presence that once felt distant or obscured by the noise of daily life. Now, through the process of communion, journaling, and meditation, the Higher Self stands as a wise and silent companion, an ever-present guide whose insights and visions continue to reveal the path ahead. This connection is no longer just a practice—it has become the guiding light by which all things are illuminated, making each decision and thought a potential for profound alignment.

In this new awareness, the seeker has also come to understand the necessity of Detachment—of stepping back from the bindings of ego, possession, and attachment. The Gnostic path has shown them how to release with grace, to live not in the accumulation of material or external validation, but in the richness of spiritual freedom. This detachment does not sever their connection with the world; rather, it opens space for a truer, deeper connection, one that is guided by wisdom and compassion rather than need or fear.

Yet, perhaps the most significant aspect of this journey lies in the connection to Service. As the seeker has transformed, there has come a natural desire to serve others, to share not just knowledge but presence, to extend the light of understanding and love. They have discovered that the ultimate purpose of gnosis is not solitary but is a radiance that seeks to touch, uplift, and heal the world. The teachings and practices encountered throughout the chapters have taught them that true power lies in love and compassion, in opening the heart to both the suffering and beauty of life.

In their synthesis, the seeker has found that each teaching, each ritual, has not only contributed to personal liberation but to a sense of unity with all beings. The Gnostic path is both the light that guides inward and the force that draws outward, bridging the personal and the universal, uniting the sacred and the mundane. Now, in every interaction, whether small or significant, the presence of the divine is known, and this recognition becomes the basis for an awakened life.

As this stage concludes, the seeker understands that the spiritual journey will continue to unfold in new ways, transcending the structured path of the book. The practices, symbols, and insights gleaned are now embedded within their consciousness, and the search for gnosis will deepen through life's evolving experiences. While each ritual once felt like a gateway, it is now simply a way of being—an approach to existence that embraces mystery, courage, and the ever-present divine spark.

Looking forward, the seeker is reminded that the journey requires vigilance and humility. It is easy, even after profound transformation, to become lost in the familiar cycles of the world. Yet they have learned that gnosis is a living fire that must be tended, a light that grows through continuous self-knowledge, reflection, and connection with the divine.

The journey synthesis stands as a testament to what is possible when one dares to turn inward, to seek not outside but within. It is the story of awakening, a timeless path walked by countless seekers through the ages. And while each path is unique, they are bound by a single truth: that within each of us lies the seed of the divine, waiting to be known, waiting to be set free.

With this final reflection, the seeker steps forward, carrying the torch of gnosis beyond the pages of teachings, rituals, and meditations, and into the boundless journey that awaits them.

Epilogue

Now that you have traveled these pages and experienced the depths of Gnostic wisdom, a new horizon opens before your perception. The journey does not end here; what you have experienced was only the first step in a continuous process, an opening that will stay with you as long as you exist. The gnosis you touched, however subtle, is a seed planted in the soil of your consciousness. Like a tree silently germinating, this knowledge will grow within you, transforming your vision, your feelings, and even the way you interpret the world around you.

The universe, once perceived only through material eyes, now reveals itself as an interconnected tapestry, a dance where the visible and invisible intertwine. Through the teachings of the Demiurge and the Pleroma, the rituals of protection and inner analysis, you have explored the vast potential of your essence, the same essence that silently pulses within you. And as you revisit the practices and reflections you have encountered here, you will realize this work is not something to "finish"; it is an inexhaustible source, a starting point for discovering your own infinity.

As you meditate, protect your energy, and allow yourself to dive into the exercises of self-analysis, you will see the veils between human and divine begin to dissolve. The concepts of separation and limitation, once so convincing, become mere illusions before the vastness of the being you now recognize within yourself. With each practice, you have the opportunity to be reborn, to transform the ordinary into sacred.

The figure of Sophia, who has accompanied you along this journey, remains as a living symbol of wisdom that rescues and elevates. Her journey is now part of yours, and her longing to reunite with the Pleroma echoes in your own soul. Every symbol explored, every concept uncovered, is a piece of a puzzle that will continue to complete itself within you—a journey where learning is not a destination, but an eternal movement.

If there is one lesson the Gnostic path leaves you, it is that the sacred inhabits every moment, every breath, and every choice. With each step you take, you draw closer to the ultimate reality, the one that transcends words and thoughts. And even if the veil of the unknown remains partially drawn, the truth of who you are—a reflection of cosmic unity—shines with greater clarity.

May you follow this inner light as a guide, always remembering that the divine is not something outside, but an eternal flame within you. May this book serve as a reminder of your ability to seek and manifest the sacred in all spheres of life.

www.ingramcontent.com/pod-product-compliance
Lightning Source LLC
LaVergne TN
LVHW040140080526
838202LV00042B/2973